TOKYO FRAGMENTS

TOKYO FRAGMENTS

Ryuji Morita   Tomomi Muramatsu
Mariko Hayashi   Makoto Shiina   Chiya Fujino

Translated by Giles Murray

IBC Publishing
Tokyo, New York, London

Published by IBC Publishing
Akasaka Community Bldg. 7F, 1-1-8 Moto-Akasaka,
Minato-ku, Tokyo 107-0051

Distributed by Yohan, Inc.
Akasaka Community Bldg. 7F, 1-1-8 Moto-Akasaka,
Minato-ku, Tokyo 107-0051

TOKYO FRAGMENTS
"TOKYO ÉLECTRIQUE"
Copyright © Tomomi MURAMATSU, Mariko HAYASHI, Ryuji MORITA,
Makoto SHIINA, Chiya FUJINO, 2000,
Directed by Corinne QUENTIN

First published in French by Editions Autrement, 2000 and in Japanese
by Kinokuniya Co. Ltd.,
English translation rights arranged through le Bureau des
Copyrights Français, Tokyo.
© IBC PUBLISHING, 2004 for the English translation.
English Translation © 2004 Giles Murray
Text editing by Laura Holland.

ISBN4-925080-88-1

Cover design by Rie ITO
Photographs by Eri IWATA

CONTENTS

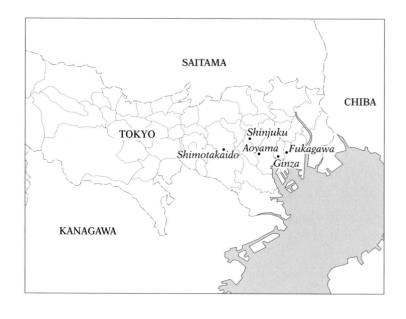

SAITAMA

CHIBA

TOKYO

Shinjuku

Aoyama Fukagawa

Shimotakaido

Ginza

KANAGAWA

Preface

With thirty-five million inhabitants, greater Tokyo ranks as the biggest urban sprawl in the world. Though a first-world city, it seems closer in scale to the chaotic mega-cities of the developing world – until one realizes that its population is actually twice that of Mexico City or São Paulo.

But what image do outsiders have of this vast city? Tokyo has no iconic architectural feature like London's Tower Bridge, New York's Empire State or Sydney's Opera House to communicate itself in shorthand to the world. Nor have foreign writers and poets felt impelled to use the place as the setting for their art as happened with imperial London or fin-de-siècle Paris a century or so ago.

It is movies, not literature, that shape our mental picture of Tokyo. The uniformed crowds surging in and out of trains in Ron Fricke's *Baraka*; the apocalyptic landscape of crumbling expressways, flickering neon and ruined skyscrapers in the animated films *Akira* or *Ghost in the Shell*; the quirky, bewildering architectural mish-mash of *Lost in Translation*: these are the sources of our stock images of the city and its various tribal groupings – the salarymen in their suits, the schoolgirls in their sailor costumes, the taxi-drivers in their white-gloves. But what film fails to provide is close-ups of specific quarters of the city and, more importantly, the individuals who live in them.

Tokyo Fragments is designed to present the microcosm

within the macrocosm; to help the reader build up a composite picture of the whole city from its constituent parts. The five stories in this book portray some of the subcultures that exist in Tokyo's various neighborhoods and so give some idea of the complexity and variety of life in a city whose population, were it a country, would place it thirty-fourth in the world, below Tanzania but above Canada.

CITY STORIES

Originally published simultaneously in French and Japanese editions, *Tokyo Fragments* forms a part of the *Romans d'une Ville* (City Stories) series of the French publishing house, Editions Autrement. The nineteen books in the series so far cover cities from Algiers to Vancouver, Havana to Shanghai. Whatever the place, the format is always the same: Five well-known writers residing in a particular city are asked to produce a short story reflecting their vision of a specific neighborhood.

The stories in *Tokyo Fragments* were commissioned by Corinne Quentin, a French literary agent who has herself lived in Tokyo for over twenty years. She deliberately selected authors who, while household names within Japan, are little known in the West. Only one of the five – Makoto Shiina – has been translated into English to date.

Having five authors of different sexes and ages – in this collection, three men, one woman and a transsexual, ranging from 42 to 64 years of age – guarantees a variety of points of view, while the stories themselves are set in locations that span the city: one in moth-eaten eastern

Preface

Tokyo; two in the glitzy central districts of Ginza and Aoyama; one in the teeming, sleazy entertainment quarter of Shinjuku; and one in the sleepy western suburbs.

THE AUTHORS

Ryuji Morita's "Fruits of Shinjuku" is set in Kabukicho, the largest of the many districts in Tokyo that specialize in selling sex. The lives of the drug-taking students, Chinese pimps and Filipina prostitutes of this story are worlds away from the safe but monotonous drudgery of the office workers who have come to personify modern Japan. Morita's story shows the uneasy, fear-tinged relationship that the Japanese have with the foreign workers who flock to Asia's wealthiest city to do the "dirty, dangerous and difficult" jobs that the locals themselves now shun.

Morita is a Tokyo native who worked as an editor at *Pia*, the Tokyo entertainment guide, before devoting himself to writing in 1996. He published his first novel, *Street Children*, in 1990 at the age of 36. Starting with the arrival of a 19-year-old country boy in Shinjuku in 1699, it recounts the lives and loves of the protagonist and his descendants over three centuries. As the title suggests, they are all streetwise characters – swindlers, kabuki actors, runaways – who live by their wits on the mean streets of Shinjuku. The story culminates with the thirteenth-generation Tetsuo fathering a child by a Filipina woman (a theme echoed in his story in this collection).

Morita's other major novel, *Bay Side Rhapsody* (1999), about a lopsided lover affair between a student and a

9

housewife twelve years his senior, is also set in Tokyo. His work, written in a terse cinematic style, has a strong sense of place and often features romantic but weak characters who lose their way when confronted with a violence they do not understand.

Tomomi Muramatsu's "Yumeko" is set in *shitamachi*, the traditional old neighborhoods of eastern Tokyo. The city's center of gravity has been shifting steadily westward since the late nineteenth century, a change hastened by the Great Kanto Earthquake of 1923 and the fire bombings of World War Two. The once-bustling heart of Tokyo is now a down-at-heel muddle of decaying wooden houses, dreary apartment blocks, small workshops and vacant lots, inhabited by a dwindling and elderly population.

It is in a *sunakku* (a sort of tiny dining-bar) in this backwater that the story of Yumeko unfolds. We are once again presented with a Tokyo quite different from the dynamic, bustling images we know from celluloid. The characters are old, barely able to eke out a living and it is never made clear if a catastrophe has really occurred, or if they are merely inventing one to bring some romance into their monotonous lives. The story may well be all smoke without fire, but it is the finely balanced ambiguity of tone that makes it so gripping nonetheless.

Born in Tokyo in 1940, Tomomi Muramatsu is the oldest writer in this collection. Originally an editor at a publishing house, Muramatsu first started to write novels under a pen name. He achieved his greatest success with his 1982 novel *The Antique Dealer's Wife* which won the prestigious Naoki prize and was adapted for theater and film. Set in Tokyo's

Shinagawa district, *The Antique Dealer's Wife* features a mysterious but attractive woman who appears from nowhere to change the lives of those she touches before vanishing once again – not unlike Yumeko herself.

Muramatsu typically prefers to let his characters reveal themselves through dialogue. "Yumeko," essentially a single long conversation studded with the reflections of the individual characters, is no exception. Muramatsu manages to be empathetic and gently mocking towards his characters at the same time, and his wry humor adds a subtle charm to his writing.

The Japanese like to think of their country as a model of social equality, unriven by differences in wealth or social class. But as Yamanashi-born **Mariko Hayashi**'s "One Year Later" shows, this is not the case: here is a world where one's position in the social hierarchy is irrevocably tied to the status of one's school, university and employer.

Eriko, a provincial girl who has moved up to Tokyo after high school seeks to make her classmates envious by collecting the trappings of big-city success. Wearing the right clothes, eating the right food, drinking at the right bars, Eriko stalks the biggest prize of all – a trophy husband – with the same materialistic single-mindedness she would devote to getting her hands on the latest must-have Louis Vuitton handbag. Of all the stories in this collection, this depiction of Tokyo as a consumer paradise is probably closest to many readers' preconceptions of the place.

Born in 1954, Hayashi worked as a copywriter before producing her first collection of essays in 1982, *Let's Go Out and Shop Ourselves into High Spirits*. She became the mouthpiece of the so-called *Hanako-zoku*, the "tribe" of young women of the 1980s who went out to work, earned money doing menial office jobs and lived according to their style bible, a lifestyle magazine called *Hanako*, often frustrating the expectations of society and their parents in the process.

Most of Hayashi's fiction deals with the "gamesmanship of relationships," and her stripped-down, uninflected style often parodies the mechanical thought patterns of her characters. In addition to her fiction, Hayashi is well known as an essayist and columnist.

Makoto Shiina's "The Yellow Tent on the Roof" is set in Ginza, Tokyo's answer to Fifth Avenue. But the protagonist has no interest in the diamonds, pricey watches and brand goods for sale around him, as he stumbles upon an alternative to the salaryman's usual lot of cramped apartments and crowded trains. Nature and solitude, he discovers, are there to be enjoyed even in the heart of the world's busiest city.

This tallies very much with Shiina's own world view. A Tokyo native, Shiina, now sixty years old, studied photography before establishing a literary magazine, *The Magazine of Books*. He published his first essay in 1979. Since then he has proved himself something of a jack of all trades: in addition to award-winning science fiction novels and photographic and cinematic accounts of his travels in Siberia, Patagonia and India, Shiina has even scripted and directed a number of feature films.

The optimistic and carefree tone of his work makes him popular with young men still reluctant to accept that the life of the corporate drone is the only valid model open to them.

Born in 1962, **Chiya Fujino** is eight years younger than any of the other authors in this collection. "The Housewife and the Police Box" deals with a claustrophobic housewife living in the suburbs. Not only is she far from the hustle and bustle of business, she is also apart from her husband, who has been posted to an office in northern Japan. Fujino is a transsexual. Not surprisingly perhaps, the characters in her books are often misfits, unable to perform the roles that society expects of them. In this story, Natsumi, the central character, is found lacking as daughter, wife and mother too. Fujino's casual sprawling prose pulls us right into the muddled heads of her characters.

Fujino worked in a publishing company until her early thirties. She has won a succession of prizes, culminating in 1999 in the Akutagawa prize – Japan's most prestigious – for *Summer Promise*, which portrays the everyday life of a homosexual couple and their transsexual neighbor.

Fruits of Shinjuku

Ryuji Morita

Shinjuku

The special on French pop music of the eighties finished, and next up was some evangelical program about Mahayana Buddhism. I switched off the radio and lit a cigarette. The room was quiet again except for the sound of Ichiro breathing in his sleep. He was still fully dressed, lying on the *tatami*, his hands clasped round his knees.

The sky finally started to whiten at four thirty-five. I picked up the Canon single-lens reflex from the desk, and pulled the curtain open halfway. Outside it had been rowdy all night but now it was as hushed as if we'd sunk to the bottom of a dam. Which room was Maria in? I peered from behind the curtain at the Hotel Silk opposite my apartment. I stood there motionless for a while, holding the camera in the hope that she would show her face in one of the windows.

I heard the faint sound of a train. Must be the first train on the outer loop of the Yamanote line. I was about to give up and step away from the window, when the emergency exit on the second floor opened. I looked through the finder and adjusted the focus on the zoom lens. A man in a black sleeveless T-shirt was holding a bottle of beer in one hand as he walked up the outside spiral staircase. One of the hotel staff maybe? Halfway up he sat down and pulled out a bottle-opener from the breast pocket of his shirt. His face was pasty, puffy. He threw back his head and started to drink straight out of the bottle. Liquid overflowed from his mouth and dribbled down his chin onto his neck. He emptied the bottle in one draught like he had to be somewhere in a hurry, then stood up and went back down the spiral staircase.

I turned to the desk and pulled open one of the drawers.

Inside were photos of Maria – nearly a hundred of the things – that I'd already taken. The first time I'd seen her was about two weeks ago at daybreak.

That morning I'd just got back from some hamburger place in Kabukicho and was smoking a cigarette by my window. I was beat from my all-night job, but didn't feel like diving straight onto my futon. I'd stubbed out my cigarette in the ashtray and pulled back the curtain. That was when the blinds of a room on the third floor of the Hotel Silk went up, and a woman showed her face.

I knew she was a pro even from a distance. At first I didn't pay any attention, but she just stood there without moving for so long that in the end I got spooked. I pulled out my camera, screwed on the zoom lens and looked through the finder. I couldn't believe what I saw.

She was a child. Her thick make-up only made her youth more obvious. With long curly hair and strong features on a darkish face, she was not Japanese. And she was crying. When I saw the tears flowing down past the corners of her mouth, I pressed the shutter without thinking. In the two weeks since then, I'd seen her go in and out of the Hotel Silk seven times.

On the other side of the wall an alarm went off, then quickly stopped.

The guy in the room next door was about twenty-five or twenty-six years old. He woke up at five every morning and left his place at five-thirty on the nose. It seemed he did a lot of road construction jobs. We sometimes bumped into each other at the public baths. He'd say hello to me with his eyes. He hardly ever spoke. I felt somehow cheered whenever I saw his buff, tan physique. Every time I saw him I thought I should start working out and get myself arm muscles and a chest like his. He had a really gorgeous girlfriend. She came over on the weekend – their routine – and would stay the night. Her ecstatic moaning would filter through my wall the whole night.

The back of my eyes ached. I put my head face down on the desk and shut my eyes. I hadn't slept enough, and my temples throbbed. Fatigue turned to particles of light that whizzed around behind my eyes. If Maria's john had been the guy in the room next door, I'd have been jealous as hell for sure, but incredibly I think I might've also slept like a baby. I was worried about Maria now and I couldn't sleep a wink.

The john who'd had his arm round Maria's shoulder when they went into the Silk last night sometime after midnight must have been about fifty years old. He was a big guy – well over two hundred pounds – and was wearing a Hawaiian shirt. I knew the bastard must be asleep now; flabby, sagging stomach and limp, dangly prick squashed up against Maria's side. He'd been plastered. I bet he'd pawed her and played with her all night long.

He'd fallen asleep while she was still astride his belly. She'd climbed off and taken a shower. Then she'd gone back to bed hoping to get some sleep, but she couldn't relax enough to manage it. He'd been the kind of customer who wakes up early and out of the blue stuffs his prick into the girl's mouth while she's still asleep and then jams a toothbrush or a bottle of body lotion inside her.

Sweat ran into my eyes and the pain forced me awake. The clock on the desk said it was past seven already. I heard a voice I recognized outside the window. I grabbed my camera and moved up behind the curtain.

I was right – it was Maria. She was in front of the hotel arguing with the big man in the Hawaiian shirt. I held my camera ready and adjusted the focus until Maria filled the frame.

She was wearing a white sleeveless minidress with a white handbag, and shiny white patent leather sandals. The outfit looked good against her dark skin. The man grabbed Maria's wrist, and I couldn't take the shot because his head was in the way. Maria pushed against his chest with her handbag and made him let go. Then she spun on her heels and walked speedily away. The man folded his arms on his chest and watched her go. I followed her retreating figure with my zoom, taking picture after picture.

The man shrugged and looked up my way. I jerked back from the window and kicked Ichiro, who was sprawled out asleep on the *tatami*, on the back of the leg.

"Let's go. We haven't been for ages," said Ichiro.

"Yeah," I nodded in reply, "It's been quite a while."

We left the apartment and walked towards Shinjuku station. We passed through the area crammed with love hotels, skirted the batting cage and turned at the corner with the police box.

In front of the twenty-four-hour hamburger joint there was a group of guys milling around. It was already past eight in the morning, but their faces looked like they hadn't had their fill of partying yet. They were trying to hit on the girls coming out of karaoke joints. One of the guys from the early morning shift who knew me a little saw me and shook his head; he looked really pissed off.

Men in suits came out in dribs and drabs from the saunas and the capsule hotels in the big buildings. They were probably salarymen from suburbs like Chiba or Saitama who'd missed the last train and spent the night to save on the taxi fare. They streamed briskly towards the station. In front of the shuttered-up game parlor a young girl – a glance was enough to tell she was a runaway – was blushing as two guys came onto her. In the square in front of the Koma Theater a few crows had swooped down and were pecking at the food in the trash. Under the covered entrance to the theater, a man with mussed-up hair sat clutching a paper bag to his chest, staring distractedly at people who were already getting in line for tickets to a musical.

"First thing in the morning and it's boiling hot," spat Ichiro.

Shut the fuck up. You're not the only one who's hot around here. I cursed him, but not aloud. If I'd opened my mouth I'd probably have started ranting and yelling all over the place.

It had been Ichiro's idea. We hadn't been for ages, but we were going to go to school – to have a good nap in a nice air-conditioned classroom. Problem was, when we got to platform thirteen at Shinjuku Station he couldn't even wait the short time it took for our Yamanote Line train to come. He'd looked at the waves of people surging across the platform, given a little sigh and gone back down the steps without saying a word. I had no choice. I followed him.

There was definitely something wrong with him. He went into a toilet stall, pulled out four bottles of Taisho Pabulon S cough syrup from the paper bag he was carrying and drained all four bottles in one go. His parents had a drug store out in Tochigi Prefecture so he knew a heck of a lot about medicine. He said that Pabulon S contained the stuff that was used to make speed, and opium was in there too.

When he first told me, I was ready to laugh it off as a not very funny joke, but he got all serious and started showing me bits of the of explanatory leaflet. He told me all earnestly how dextromethorphan, or DMX, was the key effective ingredient in most cough syrups.

Still, crazy as he was, this was the first time he'd necked down four bottles in one go. At the start, he was having a ball, saying his feet were floating up off the ground, he was flying, the ceiling was spinning, he was coming back down, etc. Then suddenly he started to groan, and crumpled down on the toilet seat. "You okay?" I asked him. "Don't shout so loud," he begged me, on the point of crying.

I stick some thinner into a plastic bag, knot up the corner and bring it up it to my mouth. Deeply, slowly I breathe in, hold it in; let my breath out little by little and do it over again. I keep doing it until I can't hear his pathetic whining anymore.

I look up at the ceiling; the neon light is sparking and flashing. A thumping sound – *bom-bom-bom-bom* – starts up in my ear. My legs feel weak. I want to crouch down. But it's too small in there for both of us to crouch. I lean back against the wall and shut my eyes, the bag still up to my mouth.

"Maria." I have a go at whispering her name. But my tongue gets tangled and she ends up as Marianna. "Marianna Marianna Marianna Marianna."

Ichiro isn't moving. I bend over him and put my hand

to his forehead. Christ, what a temperature he's got! "Hey," I say. "You all right?" That was what I meant to say, but "Heahhyullrighht?" is what comes out, all slow and stupid-sounding. I'm starting to panic and I pull his eyelids open. His eyes are bloodshot. Nothing I can do about that. I want to grab onto someone to steady myself. I've got to grab hold of some bit of me to stop myself falling over. The floor of the toilet is sinking and rising, sinking and rising. I bend and straighten my knees to ride it out. Trains keep pulling into the station; passengers try to push their way on board, twisting their bodies to slip through the closing doors. When the trains leave, the ceiling of the toilet shakes.

Keep going and never fucking stop, I shout inside my head. *A circle line train that no one can ever leave; a train that keeps going round and round forever. If the bastards really want to get off – to go to school, or go to work or whatever – they have to force the doors and throw themselves off. Nothing else for it, the passengers have to throw themselves off, one by one. Why though? What is it they're all ready to risk their lives for?*

Spit dribbles out of Ichiro's mouth, trickles down his neck. I stuff the bottle of thinner into my green shoulder bag and push out of the toilet stall. A stiff with his suit jacket under his arm passes me on his way in, opens the door, sees Ichiro crumpled up on the toilet seat and stands there, rooted to the spot. I wash my face in water from the tap, giving it a good rub.

Ichiro was out cold. I didn't know what to do with him. I stuck two fingers down his throat and made him throw up whatever he had in his stomach. I hauled him out of the

23

toilet stall. I had to get away from some station employee. The guy wasn't a cop, but had a hard-on to ask me all sorts of questions. I took a breather on the sidewalk by the south exit and then dragged Ichiro along to the promenade in front of the Takashimaya Times Square shopping complex. This took a good thirty minutes. He still looked pretty uncomfortable. He lay on the bench without moving, but sometimes he rolled his head around and squeezed out a groan.

There was a long line of customers in front of the main entrance to Takashimaya. Some young couples, but nearly all of them were women. The young mothers who'd brought their kids with them caught my eye. I suppose they were waiting for opening time. A long banner running down the façade of the building announced the summer sale.

I sat on the bench and smoked a cigarette, examining and comparing the women one by one. This was a game I really got into every time I took the train. This voice would come down to me from the sky: *Alright, you have to choose one – just one – out of all the women in this car. Then you can do whatever you want with her, but you have to make up your mind in under one minute.*

I made a quick survey of the whole car; nine women in all. I got it down to six by discounting old ladies and elementary school kids. Okay, which one to go for? A few false starts, but I get it down to three. Now there's one high school girl, one office girl in her uniform and a young mother with her baby. Right, what to do? Only twenty-five seconds left. Suddenly I start to panic.

For looks, it'd be the high school girl; the office girl's the winner in the curves category. One of the two? Hold on though. Miss this chance and who knows when I'll next have the chance to have my way with a fresh young mother. I still haven't made up my mind when the train draws into a station and all three of them get out.

Only one woman gets on and she's got to be over fifty. Bad – only five seconds left. I've got to make a split-second decision and find the youngest-looking woman out of what's left in the car. Problem is, she must be nearly forty. The train moves off and I look out of the window at the station platform. The office girl in her beige trouser-suit is sticking out her tits and swinging her hips as she walks. No doubt about it, she was the best. What the hell was I thinking?

I thought everyone played this game when they took the train, but when I mentioned it to Ichiro he looked disgusted and I asked me if I was a pervert or something.

Okay then, which one shall I go for? I was comparing two young mothers. One had on a sleeveless red blouse and white shorts that went just past her knees. The other wore a pant suit in a bougainvillea print. The line began moving before I could decide. The glass doors opened and the customers all surged into the shop together. Why did I always run out of time like this? Perhaps deep inside I didn't really want to choose just one. I was about to light up my second cigarette when I saw something that made me gasp in surprise.

Maria was sitting just three benches away from us. Her little handbag was on her knees and she was just sitting there daydreaming all by herself. The line of shoppers had hidden her till now.

"Hey, do me a favor," said Ichiro in a sleep-slurred voice. "Don't lemme fall asleep here, okay?"

Until a moment ago we'd been in the shade, but the sun had moved round and was shining directly in our faces.

"Hah, you're alive then? Tough son of a bitch, aren't you."

Ichiro laughed as he pushed himself upright. "Hey, show me your hands a minute. You're growing your nails, aren't you? In the toilet just now, those nails of yours were twisting and coiling out, getting longer and longer. Fucking freaked me out."

He stopped talking when he saw who I was looking at.

"Hey, 'what's a nice girl like you doing in a place like this,' eh? Christ, she's even better-looking than in your pictures. Go for it, dude. This is your chance."

I said nothing and just shook my head. He gave a little laugh, stuck out his chin and told me to go buy cold drinks for three. There was a vending machine a few yards away. I bought three Pepsis and handed two of them to Ichiro.

He swayed a little from side to side as he walked over and sat down next to Maria. He took a swig of his drink, then he pointed a few times first at the other Pepsi and then back at me. Maria nodded and took the can. He waved for me to come over so I walked towards them.

"You were good at English, right?" asked Ichiro.

I asked Maria if she could speak English. She shook her head and looked at Ichiro.

"*How do you do?*" said Ichiro in awkward English.

Maria just looked at him quizzically.

"First of all you should learn our names," I said.

"Good move," agreed Ichiro and started repeating our names.

"I-chi-ro…, Ry-o-ta…," repeated Maria after him.

"This is a bit embarrassing." Ichiro scratched behind his ear.

"Are you Maria?" I asked.

Her eyes opened in surprise and her expression said, "How do you know my name?" I couldn't tell her it was because I'd heard customers call her that in front of the hotel.

"Can I call you Maria?"

Maria tilted her head to one said and replied, "Okay."

"So," said Ichiro, "you do understand English after all."

"Sorry," said Maria, taking a sip of Pepsi.

"Is this cutie messing with me?" Ichiro grabbed Maria's arm. I pulled his hand off.

"She was just playing safe."

We exchanged information about ourselves for a while using a mix of gestures and clumsy English. I think we managed to get across the fact that we were living together, but there was no way we could explain we were students at a preparatory school, but that we'd lost all interest in taking the college entry exams that the school was supposed to prepare you for. A faint smile played around the corners of Maria's lips when Ichiro said that my dream was to become a photographer, and that he wanted to be a traveler, always on the move. "'*Only a traveling man…*' – know what I mean?"

What we learned about Maria was that she was from the Philippines; she'd come to Japan about three months ago; and that her big sister was here too, but she couldn't get in touch with her. That was it.

"Filipinas are pretty thin on the ground these days," said Ichiro quietly. "I thought she'd come over from Thailand or

Burma to earn herself some cash."

"Don't talk like that," I said.

"Oh I see, it's like that, huh?" And the corner of Ichiro's lips twisted up into an ironic sneer. "How then, my fine friend, should I talk?"

I said nothing. I just frowned at him.

"Don't get mad. You get mad over nothing."

Ichiro had turned back to Maria and was asking her how old she was. She looked at the ground and said nothing in reply.

"We're eighteen," I offered.

She raised her eyebrows and darted her tongue out across her white teeth. "Seventeen," she answered.

"*Okay! Seventeen!*" yelled Ichiro for no reason, and suddenly started running about. He dashed around crazily, making weird noises. The people walking along the promenade stopped in their tracks and gave him dirty looks. Perhaps it was to do with the heat. His face looked disfigured. The sight of him running jerkily around lifting his elbows and his knees up as high as they'd go – was it really so funny? A little boy began letting out high-pitched screams of delight. His mother grabbed his hand and walked him quickly away.

I urged Maria to come with me. We started walking along the promenade.

"This weather's such a drag," complained Ichiro, coming up behind us, his face completely scarlet. "You, how do you manage to look so cucumber-cool, eh?"

"Don't use hard words. Just speak regular Japanese to her. You really piss me off sometimes."

"Didn't say anything hard. What's this 'regular Japanese'

anyhow? My asshole's itchy."

Maria produced a handkerchief from her handbag and held it out to him without saying a word.

"Maria, you're a sweetie. It's too nice to spoil though," said Ichiro and he used the back of his hand to wipe the sweat from his forehead. He kept wiping, but the sweat just kept on welling up.

"Are-you-alright? Are-you-sick?"

I found myself gazing at Maria's lips as they moved.

"What?" said Ichiro. "You can speak Japanese too, huh."

Maria shrugged her shoulders.

Ichiro let out a whoop of joy the minute we got inside the Kinokuniya bookstore. The air-conditioning was so strong it gave you goose bumps. Ichiro undid the buttons of his shirt and gave a big wink to one of the girls behind the cash register. He wasn't just having a laugh though. He'd been rubbing his eyelids with his fingertips, but then he suddenly collapsed to the floor just as we reached the magazine section. His body writhed and twisted and he started to groan; in no time he was flat out, face down on the floor. His back heaved with spasms.

Maria was about to rush over when I took her arm and marched her past him. When we turned round at the photography section he was already surrounded by a crowd of rubberneckers. A sales clerk put his hand to Ichiro's forehead and announced, "He has a terrible temperature."

I started cramming whatever books I could into my dark green shoulder bag. Maria looked shocked but she said nothing. Any book would do. The staff and the customers were focused on Ichiro so nobody looked over at us. Maria pointed at an American comic book. I smiled and stuffed one with Batman on the cover into my bag. The bag quickly filled up.

Ichiro was sitting on a chair by the counter and drinking a sports drink. He must have gotten one of the staff to go buy it for him. The cash register girl was looking anxiously into his eyes. Every swig he took of the sports drink he would grab an eyeful of her large breasts and say loudly, nodding his head over and over, "I've never been to a store with such nice people." I took Maria's hand and headed for the exit. We left the store, and Ichiro came running after us.

We went down the stairs, crossed Meiji Boulevard and walked in the shadow of the office buildings. Maria said nothing but followed us. Ichiro lifted up the shoulder bag from the bottom. "Seems real heavy," he said. The rates Shinjuku second-hand bookshops paid for old books were unbelievably low, but we couldn't be bothered to catch the train to the bookstore district in Waseda.

We came out behind a junior high school. As it was the middle of summer vacation there was no sound from inside the buildings. On the playing field, the soccer and the basketball teams were running around. We went into the backyard of the school and Ichiro sat straight down on the mossy ground. It was shady and cool. I pulled the American comic out of the shoulder bag, handed it to Maria and then headed for the incinerator. Maria stood next to Ichiro, looking over at me.

I prized opened the lid with an iron bar that was lying around. Intense heat enveloped me. The smoldering garbage crackled as the flame shot up with a thin cloud of black smoke. I pulled out one book at a time from the bag and threw them into the fire. The pages lifted up, fluttered over and started to bend. They were caught in the updraft and sucked up the chimney before being completely burnt. "One book, two books," I counted, but by number ten I was tired. The last few books I just flung in all at the same time. The flames played over the cover of a book of nude photos.

It took a while for my eyes to adjust. After we'd snuck into the classroom it wasn't just Ichiro who felt dizzy, I did too. It was completely noiseless. White curtains blocked out the light.

Ichiro arranged a few desks in a row for a bed and lay down on them. He'd stuck his head into a jet of water at the drinking fountain so his hair was soaking wet. His shirt was wet too. His hands hung down limply and he was breathing through his half-open mouth. He didn't even seem to have the energy to roll over.

Maria lifted her face out of her comic and looked at Ichiro.

"Ichiro he okay?"

"Don't worry about him," I replied. "He's always like this."

Ichiro crooked his finger slightly to beckon Maria over. She put her ear to his lips.

"Will you go get me some medicine – something for a temperature?"

I asked if he had a specific drug in mind. "Yeah, good thinking," he muttered, his eyes still closed. "Shin Sedes tablets or Ronsanpo A capsules. If you can't get them, then Taisho Tonpuku."

"You're a pain in the ass."

"Well don't ask me then."

I gave a curt nod and left the building with Maria. We took a route through Tenryuji temple and out onto Meiji Boulevard to avoid the police box at Shinjuku 4-*chome*. To avoid another one at Oiwake, we went round the back of the Marui Men's building and came out on Shinjuku Boulevard. I was being more careful than necessary but I didn't want Maria being spotted by the police.

When we arrived in front of the drug store, I whispered to Maria. "Listen, I want you to speak to him in your Philippines language. What you're going to ask for is an *antipyretic*, okay?"

Maria went into the store repeating the word "antipyretic" over and over to herself.

I kept an eye on things from the street. Maria started to speak, and the pharmacist, who must have been about fifty, raised his hand and told her to hang on. He asked her if she could speak Japanese. Maria looked very earnest and just said "antipyretic." The pharmacist gave a nod of understanding, lined up a number of drugs on the counter and then opened his arms as if to say *So, which of these would you like?* Maria tilted her head to one side and playing along, said "I-chi-ro?"

I cleared my throat and marched into the shop.

"Good timing. Are you a student?" said the pharmacist to me. "Maybe you can interpret for me. I'm a bit lost."

"Can I help you?" I addressed Maria in English.

"What you saying?" replied Maria, speaking Japanese.

I acted flustered as I turned to the pharmacist. "Look, I'll find out what she needs, but could you get me something for athlete's foot? I'm in a hurry."

The pharmacist retreated into the storage area. I grabbed the box of Shin Sedes pills, took Maria's hand and hot-footed it out of there.

"You what's wrong?" asked Maria. I told her whatever happened not to look back and held her hand in my balled fist as we ran along Shinjuku Boulevard. We turned left just before the Marui Men's shop, cut through Tenryuji temple and ran straight to the junior high school's back gate.

Back in the classroom, Ichiro had fallen off the desks and lay face down on the floor. I tossed him the box of Shin Sedes pills. He flung four of them into his mouth at once. "Water," he said.

Maria gave a nod and left the classroom.

"She's a good girl." Ichiro looked at me through eyes narrowed to slits. "I'm a bit out of it, I know. But if you try anything with her, I'll never forgive you."

I shoved my hands into my back pockets and sat down on a desk.

"The state you're in, and you're still worrying about stuff like that."

"I'm serious! Not so much as a finger! Promise."

Maria came back, skating across the floor holding a cup of water. She knelt beside Ichiro, lifted his head with her hand and put the cup to his lips.

He drank the water with great satisfaction then he shut his eyes. I said nothing, just watched Maria. She was incredibly delicately built; slender arms and legs and hardly any swelling at the chest. All I could think of was her in a hotel room working away on some john, and I found it hard to breathe.

Ichiro's breathing turned regular. He was asleep.

"You only got to Japan three months ago, right?" I said. "But your Japanese is pretty good."

"I used to work in a bar in Manila called Japon," said Maria.

I was on the verge of asking her what kind of bar it was – the one she'd worked in – but I stopped myself. Maria stood up, the empty cup clutched in her hands, then sat down on a chair a little way away and put her head on the desk.

I pulled out the thinner bottle and the plastic bag from my shoulder bag and put them on the desk. Maria raised her head and looked over at me.

"Ryota hungry?"

I just shook my head and said nothing.

"Children in Manila have no food. They hungry. That's why they do thinner."

She lowered head back onto the desk.

"I've seen you many times from the window of my apartment, Maria – you going into the hotel, you coming out of the hotel. Which of the two do you think hurts me more?"

Maria's head stayed on the desk. She didn't move.

"Sorry, I shouldn't have said that."

I put my mouth to the plastic bag and breathed in thinner as hard as I could.

The noonday sun burned right directly over our heads. Heat rose from the asphalt.

We were walking with Maria between us. We had only been going five minutes when Ichiro declared he needed to take a rest. I didn't say anything. After all, he was the one who'd suggested we go to Pulp. "If we go to Pulp, there's sure to be someone there. And we can get them to buy us lunch." I was feeling uneasy about whether Maria would soon say she wanted to go home, so I went along with his idea.

Maria came to a stop in front of a shoe store. She picked up a pair of shoes from a pile in a cart by the entrance and checked out the size and the price. She said she'd promised to send a pair of leather shoes to her baby brother. She dithered and couldn't make up her mind, but finally chose a pair and started trying to negotiate a price with the sales clerk. The sales clerk says they're in the sale so he can't reduce the price, not even by a single yen. She gets mad and doesn't buy them.

We passed the front of the Shinjuku Picadilly movie theater, crossed Yasukuni Boulevard and went into the street where Shinjuku Ward office was. When we passed the infamous Furinkaikan building the atmosphere got a little bit oppressive. In this part of town you could hear people shouting in Chinese and Korean at any time of day or night.

We pushing open the door of Pulp, and we were enveloped in the cold but stale air from the air-conditioning. Ichiro was bumping into the furniture all over the place and each time he would make a solemn bow of apology to the corner of a table or chair. Sue, the *mama-san*, grimaced.

It was dark and I couldn't see that well, but I guessed that the person waving over at the end of the bar was probably Daisuke. He had his head tilted slightly to one side, his sleeves were rolled up and as he spoke he was prodding the chest of the person he was talking to with his finger. That was what Daisuke always did when he got worked up during a discussion. It was Kazuma he was talking to. Kazuma was looking down, fiddling with his empty glass.

Ichiro and I sat down at the counter on either side of Maria. Kazuma looked up as if surprised to see us and Daisuke cut short whatever he was saying and stared over at Maria.

"C'mon, introduce us," he said.

"You buy us some spaghetti, then maybe I will," replied Ichiro.

Daisuke nodded, "Okay, but just for her."

"Well, a straight talker – I like that. Thing is though, this girl's a big eater," said Ichiro before ordering three plates of spaghetti from Sue.

"Hey, hold on a minute!" protested Daisuke, but Ichiro ignored him, gulped down a full glass of water and got up to go to the bathroom.

Daisuke had come over and was sitting next to Maria. She grinned at him, "Hello."

"I know – I've seen you on TV," replied Daisuke. "No wait – maybe it was in a fashion magazine."

"Has your friend been taking drugs again?" asked Kazuma.

"Hey," I smiled back at him. "Let's not pretend we're talking some big dirty secret here. You can call them drugs, but it's all just drugs like you buy at the local pharmacy."

Daisuke's arm had crept round the back of Maria's chair and he was whispering something into her ear. Some crap like "You're beautiful" or "Your eyes are a well of passion," I supposed. I was tormented, waiting to see how Maria would react. Next Daisuke held her hand in his. "The hand of an angel," he said. It set my teeth on edge.

Ichiro came back from the bathroom. He looked a bit better.

"You just behave yourself, okay," warned Sue.

"Yeah, sorry," said Ichiro, drawing his head in between his shoulders. "I've thrown up and I feel a lot better now. I'm a big boy. I can take care of myself. No need to worry about me. I'm okay. No worries."

"Don't worry. No one's worrying about you," said Kazuma, mimicking Ichiro's way of speaking. "Nobody gives a fuck about a loser like you."

Sue put the plates of spaghetti on the counter. They were glistening with oil. You couldn't say a word against the spaghetti here. I started shoveling it into my mouth. "This is great. Mmm."

Maria shut her eyes and placed her palms together in prayer before she picked up her fork.

"Where did you pick this one up then?" asked Daisuke.

I ignored him. "How about a coffee?" Sue asked Maria. "And don't worry, it's on the house."

Maria happily agreed. I continued to eat my spaghetti in silence. I polished off my plate in no time, and since Ichiro wasn't eating his I set to work on his plate too.

"Ryota, where'd you pick her up, eh?" Daisuke asked a second time.

"Got any money on you?" I asked Maria.

She nodded and pulled a ten thousand yen note out of her bag.

"We don't need you to pay for our stupid lunch, okay."

Daisuke clicked his tongue angrily, then got up and went back to his original seat at the far end of the room.

"First time for me to have such good coffee," said Maria in English

Sue could speak Cantonese and English on top of Japanese. She and Maria started chatting energetically across the counter. Maria's English was shit – a whole lot worse than Sue's. I was in a great mood. I licked my plate clean, right down to the film of oil that had formed on its surface. Sue looked over to me.

"Will you give me a hand here? Then you can have the spaghetti for nothing."

I nodded and went in behind the counter. Looking over at Maria from time to time, I washed the dishes, broke up ice with an icepick and folded paper napkins.

Sue changed the station of the cable radio and came back behind the counter.

"That girl – could be dangerous, you know," she whispered. "When did you meet her? Today was it? Ask her if she has her passport or not. Usually they've had them taken away. What are you planning to do, Ryo-chan? Better for you not to get deeply involved. But she's a pretty girl, really pretty. Fallen for her? But it's bad news. She's bound to have some no-good pimp behind her. Do you know if she's run away? You should ask her. But take my word for it, working girls mean trouble."

The door opened and some more customers came in. With the light behind them all I could see was their silhouettes, but it was a group of three girls. From either side of him, Daisuke and Kazuma slapped Ichiro heartily on the thighs. "The tall one, the one in the miniskirt – she's mine. What about you?"

"Me? I'll take the one with highlights".

"No two ways about it. I'll have the one in the camisole," declared Ichiro.

The three of them beckoned. The girls paused in the doorway and had a powwow. Then they came directly towards them.

"Three of you, three of us: perfect," said the girl in the miniskirt.

"Well, well, what a coincidence" Daisuke replied.

They moved over to a table and Maria was left sitting at the counter alone. I winked at her. She shrugged her shoulders and smiled.

"A Singha for me," said the girl with highlights. And the other two chimed in with "same here."

I got the Thai beer out of the refrigerator and took it over to their table. They started talking noisily. Daisuke, Kazuma and Ichiro were smiling at the girls they had each selected and ignoring the other two.

"You don't drink then?" asked the girl in the camisole. She had an unusually high-pitched voice. Ichiro clapped a Sedes A tablet into his mouth, said "pardon me" and took a swig of her beer.

"See, I'm drinking aren't I?"

"That's not what I meant. Anyway, listen. I'm flat broke right now. How about buying this member's card? It's for a club in Roppongi, a really fancy, top-class joint, with bunny-girls and everything."

"Oh yeah, right. I'm supposed to believe that a young girl like you paid your own money to join a club like that for dirty old men."

"That's a mean way to talk to me. But actually you're right – my ex-boyfriend became a member and then gave me the card. It's good for another two months – worth fifteen thousand. Yours for only three thousand."

"Come on, if you need money you can get the old-timers at the club to fork out."

Ichiro slid his arm around the waist of the girl in the camisole.

"Yeah, girls like you, you're charging, what – ten thou a pop to jerk someone off or blow them?"

The girl in the camisole squealed, "What kind of girls do you think we are? We'd never do anything like that."

The three girls shook their heads in denial, then put their heads together for a little conference before crying out, "That's the sort of thing that high-school girls do."

I poured the last of the coffee from the jar of the vacuum brewer into Maria's cup. "Christ, they're annoying," I complained. Maria shook her head. "Me, I enjoy."

"So who are you?" the girl in the miniskirt asked me. "You don't work here, do you?"

I shrugged and said nothing.

"Your friend, she's really gorgeous. Can she speak Japanese?"

Daisuke said something to the girl. If you ever saw him speaking about something energetically, he was most likely badmouthing somebody.

"Does she work as a model?" asked the girl with highlights.

"Her make-up's professional standard, but no, she's not a model," Daisuke replied.

"So what is she then?" persisted the girl in the miniskirt.

Daisuke whispered something into her ear. She nodded.

"Now you, sweetie," he continued. "You could rent

yourself out for a good sum." Daisuke brushed his hand over her thighs.

"No touching, you dirty old perv!" she protested, clinging to his arm. "How much could I sell myself for?"

"Hey, Ryota," Daisuke said to me. "How much did she cost you?"

I filled a glass up with water and came out from behind the counter. I stood in front of Daisuke. I didn't say anything. I threw the water straight into his face. "What the hell are you doing?" Daisuke stood up.

"That's not very nice," said the girl in the miniskirt.

"Let's get out of here," I said to Maria. Maria apologized to Sue.

"No problem," returned Sue.

When Maria climbed down from her stool at the counter, Ichiro announced that he was leaving too.

"Hey wait a minute," said the girl with the highlights. "Are you kidding? That leaves three girls and two boys. What are we supposed to do?"

I grabbed Maria's hand and we left the bar together. Outside, she stopped. "What's wrong?" I asked. But she just stood there without moving, hanging her head.

Ichiro came out. He'd gone all pale again.

"Having fun are you, wrecked on your Sedes?"

In response, Ichiro just shook his head. "Shouldn't have passed up on a girl like that," and he grinned at Maria, showing his broken tooth.

Back in the apartment, Ichiro collapsed onto the futons, which we hadn't bothered to fold up and put away. When Maria spotted the Hotel Silk on the other side of the street, she pouted. "Me, I'm going," she declared.

"How much?" I asked. "How much do I have to pay for you to stay with me?"

Maria shook her head weakly. "Japan man, always money, give money. 'I love you, I love you now take it, take money.' That how you are."

"That's not it. How much money have you got to make tonight? How much do I need to pay you for you to spend the time with me?"

Maria grabbed my arm and looked at my watch. It was just before four.

"Me, Ryota, have little bit of time, okay."

"God, it's so hot," moaned Ichiro.

Maria nodded her agreement. She took a towel down from a hanger and went into the kitchen. She wet the towel, came back and started wiping Ichiro's face. He was sweating freely all over. She made him take off his T-shirt and jeans and used the towel to wipe his chest, his stomach and his thighs. His boxers were bulging. I laughed and Maria laughed too. Ichiro had shut his eyes and seemed to be relaxing when suddenly he seized Maria's wrist and pushed her hand down into his boxers. Her hand stuck in his waistband, she looked over at me. I ripped off my cotton pants and pushed my swollen briefs into her face.

Maria removed her hand from Ichiro's boxer shorts and stood up in silence. She kissed me lightly on the cheek and got ready to leave the apartment.

"Where are you going?"

"Shopping, dummy," she replied with a laugh.

I followed her out of the apartment.

The supermarket was really crowded. Maria nimbly

slipped in between people and made her way to the back of the shop. I told her I didn't have any money. "Okay, I have money," she answered. I walked along behind her holding the basket.

When Maria discovered the avocados and kiwis she squeezed my arm in delight. The basket quickly filled up with fruit: mangos, papayas, bananas, lemons.

"No way we can eat all that" I told her.

Maria shook her head in disagreement and smiled.

"I have money. No problem. Ichiro – he eat fruit, he feel better."

Three women the wrong side of forty walked by and openly gave us the dirtiest of looks. Maria didn't pay the slightest bit of notice. She saw a big red snapper, and let out a shriek of excited delight. "I'll buy. That one." Looking at her profile as she solemnly selected her fish, I thought to myself how happy I'd be if I could marry her.

Maria pulled five ten thousand yen notes out of her bag and put one of them on the counter. The check out girl scanned Maria's face, then looked at me out of the corner of her eye. That fifty thousand had to be the money she'd been paid by last night's client.

"What's wrong with you?" Maria asked. "You make angry face."

I shook my head and rubbed my face with both hands.

When we got back to the apartment, Ichiro had spread Maria's photos like playing cards all over the futon and was examining them. Maria crouched down over the bedding and picked one up.

Still holding the shopping bag, I was standing in the doorway.

"Ryota took 'em," said Ichiro.

"You crazy," shouted Maria and she started to tear them up one at a time.

I watched in silence. Finally unable to stand anymore, I picked up a close-up of her face and begged her please not to rip up that one. Maria was looking at the floor, but she nodded weakly then headed for the kitchen. I asked her if there was anything I could do to help out but she didn't reply. "Use this instead of an apron," I said and I made her put on a T-shirt over her white dress.

Maria boiled the red snapper, the avocados, the kiwis and the lemons in a pan. I washed the rice and set the rice-cooker. In no time at all, the apartment was filled by an overpowering smell.

The dish Maria made was too heavy and didn't do much for my appetite. Ichiro put the fish on top of his rice, then poured a cupful of water over it all to wash it down. Once he'd finished that off, he plucked a banana off the bunch and dived back onto his futon. Maria watched me intently as I ate.

"Very good," I said.

She raised her eyebrows. "Maybe."

It took me a while, but I managed to empty my plate. Ichiro was already snoring gently in a contented sleep. After Maria had finished the washing up, she announced, "I go now." I got to my feet, tongue-tied. Maria turned around, her hand on the doorknob and said, "Goodbye Ichiro."

When we got out of the apartment I held her hand. When I put an arm around her shoulder, she leaned her head on my chest. Her hair smelled of avocados.

We stopped in front of an old building. "What's wrong

with you"? Maria asked. I didn't say anything but just led her by the hand into the entrance hall. The janitor's room was empty. I pulled her over to the bottom of the stairs and put my hand around her waist. I pulled her up against me and thought that her slender waist might snap. I shut my eyes and gently put my lips to hers. She froze. When I took my lips away, a small sigh escaped her lips.

"Maria, I don't want you to go."

"My boss – he dangerous," she said. "I get in trouble. You want that?"

I said nothing, but shook my head.

"Goodbye. I enjoyed. You, Ryota, and Ichiro – good people."

With a twist of her body, Maria slipped out of my arms.

"I want to get to know you better. What should I do?"

Maria gave a little nod and pulled a business card out from her handbag. A mobile phone number was printed beneath characters that read "With our love."

"Cost high. Is okay for you?" said Maria, showing her white teeth in a grin as she walked off towards Okubo Station.

I took out all my savings from the ATM machine at the bank. I thought I had about forty thousand yen; in fact I only had twenty-eight thousand. There was three thousand four hundred and seventy in my wallet. That was all the cash I had.

When I got back to the apartment, Ichiro was still fast asleep. I hardly dared to breathe as I pulled the wallet out from the back pocket of his jeans. There were only two one thousand yen bills in it. I slipped out the two bills and replaced the wallet in his pocket. I then shoved my camera into the shoulder bag and left the apartment again.

I pushed through the shop-curtain of the pawnbroker's. I'd been here before with Ichiro. We'd swiped a watch that someone had left behind in one of the school classrooms, brought it here and swapped it for four one thousand yen notes. We'd spent the money necking beers and scarfing giant hamburger steaks. The manager picked up my camera. The body was old, he said, so he would give me ten thousand for that, but he'd give me twenty thousand for the zoom. The lens had cost me sixty thousand yen, but what choice did I have? I said goodbye to the lens and took the twenty thou in return.

I went into a phone-box, and punched in the number on the card. After a single ring, the phone was picked up. "Yes?" came the low voice of a woman.

"I want a session with Maria, please."

"Thank you for calling. Your membership number, please." The woman spoke like a pre-recorded message.

"This is the first time I've called."

"Please hold the line."

A little tune played while I waited. After a while a man's voice said, "Sorry to keep you waiting. We always ask first-time customers to formally register as members."

"Register?"

"We'd like you to come to our offices so we can explain our system to you. We don't ask for a membership fee. Please be assured on that point."

The man's voice was gentle and polite.

"By the way, how did you hear about Maria?"

I managed to stammer out that I'd heard about her

through a friend.

"Ah, of course, so it's a recommendation."

The man paused a moment and then asked if I would be able to come around soon.

I replied I'd be quick and hung up. I followed the route the man had given me on the phone, turning at the corner where the Taiwanese restaurant was, going out onto Shokuan Boulevard, passing the Korean food store and taking a left just past the boxing gym. I found the brown eight-floor apartment block no problem.

There was no nameplate or plaque of any kind on the door of Apartment 801, the place he'd specified. I rang the bell, the door opened and a woman in a bright dress the color of orange sherbet stuck her head out. Her hair was tied in a ponytail with a band in the same orange.

"I'm the guy who called a moment ago."

The woman nodded and pulled open a curtain that partitioned the space. There were seven or eight girls seated in a six-*tatami* mat room. I quickly looked them over, but Maria wasn't there.

The room I was shown into was dimly lit. A butterfly tapestry on the wall and some seashell knick-knacks caught my eye.

A man was sitting on a sofa. He was dressed like a student in black pants and a white shirt. He was delicately built and pale – the sort of man whose age isn't easy to guess. Looking at his boyish face you'd think he was about twenty, but his hugely self-assured expression belonged to a man over thirty.

He indicated an armchair with his chin. I sat down facing him.

"Thank you for coming. Were you able to find us easily?"

He was just as polite and formal as on the telephone. I said nothing, just nodded.

"Right. I should like to charge you sixty thousand yen for this afternoon."

"What! What are you talking about?"

"I think you know perfectly well what I'm talking about." He smiled. His smile looked as though it were pinned to his cheeks.

"I was going to ask you for two or three hundred thousand, but I changed my mind. What's the point in threatening a child like you? I'll just charge you for two short sessions."

"I'm sorry but I really don't know what you're talking about."

"Really? You don't know what I'm talking about? You Japanese students are really not too bright."

The man turned to the door. "Aileen," he called out.

The door opened. The woman in the orange dress came into the room, pushing Maria ahead of her.

"What's this about a charge for the afternoon?"

Maria suddenly fell to her knees in front of the man.

"This man he do nothing. My fault."

"He didn't do anything?" asked the man. "Aileen, what's this about?"

The woman leaned forward and spoke into Maria's ear. "You must have at least let him kiss you, eh?"

Maria raised her head and nodded, touching her lips with a finger.

"That's how it is," said the man, and he turned back to face me. "You will pay us sixty thousand yen. The fifty thousand for tonight will, of course, be on top of that."

I pulled opened my wallet and poured its contents out onto the table.

"Fifty-one thousand four hundred and seventy. That's all I've got, not one cent more."

The man gave a sinister smile. "You're a little naïve, my friend. You may not have enough, but that's not the end of it – not in this world."

The telephone rang and Aileen picked it up.

"Thank you for calling. Your membership number, please." She jotted down a mix of letters and numbers in a notebook. "I'll send her along in a minute," she said and hung up the phone. "Maria, someone's asked for you. A shortie."

"Hold on a minute. I was first."

I took my camera out of the shoulder bag.

"It's a bit of an old model, but I paid seventy grand for it."

The man's hand shot out and grabbed hold of my shirt collar.

"I'm an overseas student at a university here in Tokyo. I'll be a post-grad next year, so I don't want to make any waves. But there's plenty of people working for me who'll kill without a second thought. They'll break your shoulder for thirty thousand; they'll slice up your face for a hundred thousand; pay them three hundred grand and they'll pluck out your eyes and dump your body in the Saitama mountains. Now, what are you going to do about making up the rest of the money? Sort it out with Aileen, okay?"

As he finished speaking, he put a hand on Maria's waist, then left the room.

When the door had shut behind him, Aileen gave a vigorous nod. "You're lucky. Today he was very kind to you. Thank God."

I stood there, rooted to the spot. The telephone rang. Aileen picked it up. "Oh, I'm sorry," she said. "But she is with a customer at the moment. We have many other pretty girls. What kind do you like? Well how about Jocey then? Yes, she's the same age as Maria. She's not broken in in yet, you know, so you'll need to be gentle or she'll start crying. Thank you, I'll send her right along."

She hung up the phone, relayed the message to the next-door room and quickly came back.

"Maria's our most popular girl. Japanese men love girls of mixed blood. Girls with Latin blood are popular, you know. But when I see Maria she reminds me of my daughter. It makes me sad."

"You're a mother?"

"Yes, I am. I've got two kids. I'm going to work here for two more years then I'm going home. Till then it's grin and bear it.

"Aileen, if I want to marry Maria what do I need to do?"

When I said that, her expression became gentle suddenly, as if somebody had loosened a screw.

"What are you saying! You know you've got to wait three years."

"Three years?" I echoed. "Is that how long her contract is or something?"

"No, nothing like that. But the Philippines and Japan are the same. You can't get married if you're only thirteen years old."

The telephone rang again and Aileen answered. *You can't get married if you're only thirteen years old*: I repeated the words to myself. Aileen kept nodding and bowing into the receiver. The expression on her face became visibly grimmer and she tutted when she hung up the phone.

"Maria's run away. You, get out of here. Him, he's dangerous when he gets angry. He'll kill you." Aileen opened the door as she was speaking.

"What about the rest of the money?" I asked.

She said nothing and just shook her head.

I stuffed the camera into my shoulder bag, and fled out of the apartment building.

I gasped for air as I ran through the nighttime streets. I saw Colombian streetwalkers and Bolivian hookers and Iranian pimps. Cars stuck in traffic kept on hooting their horns and a group of boys had formed a circle round a tottering, wasted salaryman and were beating him up. In front of a Korean street stall selling chicken feet, men in sandals were sharing a cigarette butt and drinking.

I went across Shokuan Boulevard into Kabukicho. Asian and South American girls were parading their smiles in front of a building crammed full of tiny sex clubs. Suzie Wong dresses slit right to the tops of their thighs; pink dresses with the sleeves puffed out like butterfly wings; black stockings and white high-heeled pumps; skirts that spread like upturned bowls; dresses showing glimpses of shoulders and breasts...

An expensive imported car was parked in front of a Chinese club. Men in dark suits were getting out of it. In a panic, I slipped into a back alley. Where would Maria have run to? Perhaps she was cowering in the junior high school classroom. Maybe she was hunched up on a bench on the promenade.

As I threaded my way through the drunks, her face came back to me. But the face I saw was the sad, lonely-looking face of the time I first took her picture. With my zoom, I'd gotten a close-up of her face as she looked out of the hotel window. It was the picture I had begged her not to rip up, the one with Maria gazing vacantly towards the camera.

I charged into the apartment, and leaned back against the door with my hand on the doorknob, trying to catch my breath.

"What's wrong with you?" Ichiro looked up. He was leaning over the table eating a papaya. "Don't tell me that you went ahead and did it without me?"

I went into the kitchen and drank water straight from the tap. I then stuck the nape of my neck under the strong stream to cool off. I thought that Maria could make her way here to the apartment. But that was just a way out for me and my gutlessness. Some of the men I'd passed as I was running through Kabukicho had been speaking Chinese: I'd cringed with fear when I heard them.

"So where've you been all this time?"

I didn't reply but sat down at the table. I picked up a papaya and a mango in each hand and bit into them hard. They gave off a faint smell of blood.

Yumeko

Tomomi Muramatsu

Fukagawa

*I*t was not that dark in the bar, so perhaps it was the fault of the smoke-grimed wall behind the counter that Genji seemed to melt away into a blended background of brown and black.

When the last person arrived that would be all of them, but there were still ten minutes to go before the arranged meeting time. The plan was to get underway only once everyone had arrived, so the three who had come early were at a loose end, and just gazed into the middle distance.

The owner of the Fukagawa Bar said he'd give them all a beer, but Yamaguchi stopped him with a wave of his hand. It was then that Genji struck a match. They all found themselves staring at the tips of Genji's fingers where a flame had come into sudden being in the darkness.

At first, the flame of the match flared up wildly, but in no time it had changed to a calm, orange-tipped flicker of blue that slowly crawled up the shaft towards Genji's fingers. He drew the flame up as close to the tips of his fingers as he could bear before blowing it out with a single puff. The shaft of the match continued to burn, went red and twisted out of shape; it then turned to ash, dropped into the ashtray and metamorphosed into cinders before their eyes. The part of the shaft left in Genji's fingers flared red and faded. Then it too began to twist into a spiral, shrinking as it hardened.

Genji flicked the match into the ashtray, a conflicted expression on his face. Everyone else had been watching the match with the same intensity as Genji, but they heaved a collective sigh of relief when they saw the cindered remnants curled up in the ashtray.

Gonbei, who was sitting next to Yamaguchi, tilted his head and looked a little puzzled. "Hey, I thought you quit smoking?"

"That's right," added the bar owner. "It's over a year now since the doc told Gen to stop smoking. He was so impressed you know, Gen managing to quit like that."

As he said this, the owner of the bar was looking at Yamaguchi as if seeking confirmation from him.

Yamaguchi remembered very clearly when Genji had made the painful announcement at this same counter about a year and a half ago that the doctor had issued a warning and he was going to quit smoking. Yamaguchi had been watching what Genji was doing without paying much attention. But it was indeed odd for Genji to strike a match, given that he was supposed to have stopped smoking.

"Look," began Genji, sensing that he was the center of attention and speaking with something like a sigh, "I didn't smoke because I liked it, you know."

"But the doctor said you were an incredibly heavy smoker," retorted Gonbei with his lips pursed and his expression defiant. Gonbei's real name was Taro Suzuki, but in this bar he went by the name of Gonbei.

At first Yamaguchi had thought this was because he managed an *izakaya* dining-bar called Gonbei. But in fact, it seemed that he had taken the name because, while the courtesans of the old Yoshiwara pleasure district took euphemistic nicknames called "Genji-names," the courtesans of the Fukagawa area referred to their pseudonyms as "Gonbei names."

You may sell your art, but you must never sell your honor: This was the attitude unique to the geisha of this area, the so-called Fukagawa or Tatsumine geisha, who had taken such great pride in their arts and skills. Apparently the geisha liked to give themselves men's names such as Miyokichi, Adakichi, Yonekichi or Mojiriki. Gonbei declared that he hated both the name "Taro" and the name "Suzuki" because they were the commonest names in the country. So he had given himself the nickname Gonbei with the intention of carrying on the spirit of the Fukagawa geisha.

Yamaguchi could understand Gonbei's motivation for the name change, considering this area by the Onagi river with its center in Monzen-nakacho had once been the flourishing Fukagawa red-light district.

"But Suzuki, don't you see that what you're doing is basically giving yourself a pseudonym – Gonbei – that means 'pseudonym' in the first place?" protested the owner of the Fukagawa Bar, pouring cold water on the idea. The other regulars also disapproved on the grounds you shouldn't be embarrassed of the name your parents had given you, but Gonbei refused to capitulate.

"Here in this bar I would like you to address me as Gonbei, please," he declared, then bowed exaggeratedly low to make clear just how strongly he felt about his whim. Gonbei was a business man in his mid-thirties. Why he felt such an attachment to Fukagawa remained a mystery, but in this bar at least the nickname Gonbei had taken root. This was the person who had gotten worked up and was now needling Genji. Maybe it was an example of his intention to carry forward the spirit of the Fukagawa geisha. Yamaguchi leaned forward to hear how Genji would respond.

"I never smoked because I liked the taste of tobacco." Genji spat out the curt reply, as if rebuking Gonbei. Gonbei in turn stared back at him with an expression that said

"What the hell kind of an excuse is that?"

"I smoked because I like striking matches."

The room was silent.

"When you strike a match, first a flame flares up, then the flame moves slowly along the shaft, ever so slowly. The thing is though, the flame has infinite forms of expression."

"Expression, huh?"

"And then the shaft turns bright glowing red as it burns. Then it contorts itself and bit by bit starts to disintegrate. That's a sight I can't get enough of."

"A sight, you say?"

"The part of the match that you hold in your fingers stays white and it's only the end that goes black. I feel that tells us something. If you carefully put the unburned part in the ashtray, you get a single match stuck to the bottom of the ashtray: its color and its shape may have changed, but it somehow seems as if the pieces want to put themselves together again... That's an amazing sight too."

"So what you're saying, Genji, is that you used to smoke just to contemplate the match?"

"Yes, that's what I'm saying."

"So it was the match, not the cigarette, that had the starring role?"

"Anything wrong with that?"

"No, nothing in particular wrong with that...but – I don't know – maybe it's unfair to the cigarette. The cigarette is reduced to insignificance."

"No. It has an important supporting role."

"But it's the cigarette that's the star – the match should be playing second fiddle."

"Well personally, I think it's the other way round."

"Which means that you really did smoke all those years just to see the match burning?"

"Exactly. And that's since I was fifteen, so that's a fifty-five-year smoking career."

"Fifty-five years! That's not just a habit, that's pyromania!"

Gonbei shook his head in disbelief. Genji had never revealed this to Yamaguchi and the other two before, either. Yamaguchi suspected that the whole thing might be a typical Genji joke. He could have cooked up the story as a way of getting back at the doctor who had forced him to stop smoking after so many years. That was very much the kind of thing Genji would do. But the story could be true: it felt plausible enough for that.

That's the kind of person Genji is after all…

As Yamaguchi was saying this to himself, the door opened and Yasuhara came into the bar. Yasuhara had a small clothes shop on the other side of the Onagi river from the Fukagawa Bar. He was a custom tailor, and his business was making bespoke suits in an old style that had nothing to do with contemporary fashion. Lately, the only diehards who continued to order clothes from Yasuhara were a couple of old men who had been customers for over twenty years. There was no way that adjustments and invisible mending were enough to keep the business going. Their only daughter had married and moved out a long time ago, and no one really knew how the couple earned enough to live on. Perhaps, Yamaguchi mused, not being in the middle of town meant they didn't need to pay rent and that was what was saving them.

"Right, now we're all here…" began Yamaguchi, with

an air of taking charge. For a moment Genji, Yasuhara, Gonbei, and the owner of the Fukagawa Bar all looked very serious. The three who had been summoned by Yamaguchi had no idea what the meeting was about. They had imagined it was just going to be all the regulars having a drink together, so they had turned up in a relaxed frame of mind. But there was something unusual about the look in Yamaguchi's eye, and they tensed up accordingly.

"So Yamaguchi, do you want our advice about something?" inquired Gonbei, wrinkling his brow. The other three gave a similar inquisitive frown and stared at Yamaguchi. He smiled ruefully, took a sip from the glass of whiskey and water in his hand, and looked at each of them in turn.

"Just supposing –" he began, then fell silent.

"Come on, Yamaguchi, spit it out. Stop being so stand-offish. Got yourself a young girlfriend? I'm more than happy to give you a few pointers. Yes, if that's what the problem is, leave it all to me."

"You're jumping the gun, Genji. It's not healthy for old men to rush to conclusions."

"Hmm, never heard that one before. So I suppose you want to talk about divorcing your wife then?"

"No, actually. It's not about me at all."

"So is it Gonbei here who's been hoodwinked by some broad?"

"I told you Genji, stop trying to guess what's coming. First guess or second guess, you're still completely off the mark."

"Alright then, Mister Gonbei, why don't you tell us what you think this is all about. What does Yamaguchi need our advice for?"

"I've already told you: it's not directly to do with me."

"But you can't deny that advice is advice."

"Well no, but..."

"It's because you're beating around the bush and being all mysterious that Genji's off jumping to conclusions," chimed in the bar owner with an ingratiating smile. Running a bar called Fukagawa, he was just as passionate a believer in the Fukagawa district as Gonbei. The owner's belief was bolstered by a strong conviction that a miraculous spirit of human kindness hovered over the neighborhood. Whenever he got the chance, he would propound his theory that it was the river that engendered this spirit; a moist, damp kindness of a sort peculiar to reclaimed land.

"Okay, I can accept the idea of a river being 'kind,' but what on earth is this 'kindness of reclaimed land'?" a middle-aged customer had once asked, his head cocked skeptically at the owner's theories. The owner had tutted and given the customer a look of utter contempt.

"Well, people who don't get it – I mean people who don't understand this kindness – they really don't get it. This place used to be sea. It was filled in, and so the land is saturated with the kindness of the sea."

"So what you're saying is that for you, water – whether it's a river or the sea – is kind and gentle."

"Am I wrong?"

"No, I'm not saying you're wrong."

"They filled in a place which was originally sea and they called it 'Fukagawa.' Fukagawa means 'deep river,' so the area became what's called an *okabasho*."

"An *okabasho*?"

"So you don't know what that is either, huh?" At which point the manager sighed deeply, shook his head, and subjected the middle-aged customer to a hard stare.

In the Edo period, the Yoshiwara or licensed red-light district flourished as the greatest pleasure ground in the City of Edo. It prospered so much that there was a saying that the only places in Edo which had a turnover of a thousand ryo were the riverside fish market in the morning, the playhouse in the daytime, and the Yoshiwara by night. But if you went out in the Yoshiwara, as you might expect you had to do things according to certain rules. These complicated procedures eventually acquired a certain kind of prestige; the customers got some of their satisfaction from the elevated status of the pleasures they enjoyed there. That was how the Yoshiwara red-light district worked.

But there was no doubt that some customers felt all the troublesome rules and rituals were a nuisance. They felt that going out in the Yoshiwara was boorish and unrefined; that a more stylish kind of fun could be had in the Fukagawa unlicensed quarter. Though not sanctioned by law, the existence of this other red light district was tacitly accepted. It was called an *okabasho*, or unlicensed pleasure quarter. The bar owner was convinced the reason that the Fukagawa unlicensed district had been no less lively than the official Yoshiwara during the Edo period was because it wasn't overgrown with formalized rules: it offered a world where people could do whatever they felt like doing.

"You see, the pronunciation of *okabasho*, or 'unlicensed quarter,' conceals the word *akubasho*, 'wicked place.' At least, that's what I like to think."

The way in which the owner delivered this remark made

it quite clear that he was convinced the customer would never be able to understand anything he said.

"That must mean then that the customers of the Yoshiwara were of a higher class?"

"In the opinion of people who regard that sort of thing as being higher class, yes."

The customer said nothing.

"Let me put it like this: the Yoshiwara clientele included a lot of people of the warrior class, but Fukugawa played host to lots of city people and not many samurai. People who were prejudiced and looked down on city merchants had no right to come here to Fukagawa for their fun."

"That makes sense. But does that feeling still exist here even now?"

"Well, times change. The pleasure quarter has vanished, but I think you can sometimes catch a whiff of the old atmosphere."

Silence.

"And you can still sense that there is water down there underneath this reclaimed land."

"I wonder..."

"You feel it or you don't – it's down to whether you have the ability to perceive these things or not."

More silence.

"But it's hopeless for someone who doesn't even know what an *okabasho* is. Myself though, I feel that the land around here is a sort of stage on water."

"Meaning?"

"Meaning a stage or set that's been built on top of water. And I can tell you that all sorts of plays are still being acted out on that stage."

"What, even now?"

"Yes, even now, here in this part of town you have a bunch of people behaving like actors."

"You think so, huh?" The expression of the middle-aged customer made clear that he was no longer able to follow the owner's somewhat obsessive train of thought. Yamaguchi, however, who had been listening to their exchange from one end of the bar, somehow felt that he understood what the owner (or "Master" as they all called him) was getting at.

Yamaguchi managed a jazz-café called Step not far from the Fukagawa Bar. Maybe "managed" is the wrong word, as it wasn't at all clear whether his jazz-café was really a going concern. Yamaguchi would try to be there as much as possible from about eleven o'clock on weekday mornings until seven o'clock when the place shut. But it was only once or twice in the course of the entire year that all the tables were occupied. Most days, about four or five sets of customers would come in, and days when not even one customer showed up were fairly common.

The fact that he was nonetheless able to make a living of sorts was, just as with Yasuhara's clothes shop, only because he did not have to pay rent. When the city of Tokyo was flailing after the collapse of the eighties' bubble economy, businesses in the old *shitamachi* districts were only able to survive because the shops there were built not on rented land, but on land owned outright and handed down through generations. In Fukagawa, perhaps the same old businesses could keep going precisely because the old atmosphere of a century ago still lingered there, mused Yamaguchi. The way he thought about things had much in common with the owner of the Fukagawa Bar.

A jazz-café, he could not help feeling, was hardly a perfect match with the Fukagawa district. But then again, he believed that the temperament of the ordinary folk of old Edo was closer to jazz than the cramped and restrictive existence of modern Japan. When Yamaguchi pulled out a record from the shelf in the empty café and listened to a skit of an old-fashioned vaudeville headliner he felt sometimes that he was experiencing an atmosphere unique to a Fukagawa jazz-café.

Yamaguchi had been running Step for nearly thirty years now and had never once turned the amplifier off. It was Genji who had first expressed his doubts about that. People said that Genji had been an actor, but no one was sure. There was also a rumor that he had been a famous transvestite performer, which seemed more likely to be true. Be that as it may, Genji had a keen eye for other people's play-acting. He must already have been in his late sixties, but his interest in people was keener than average. Yamaguchi might say that he had never turned off the amplifier, but no one had seen the interior of Step in the nighttime. And since it was Yamaguchi who got there first in the morning, Genji argued, there was no proof to back up his claim.

"Let me ask you..." Yamaguchi began, looking gravely back at Genji. "Gen, tell me: when you go to bed, do you turn off your heart and stop breathing before going to sleep?"

Genji said nothing.

"The amplifier is to a jazz-café what the heart is for a human being."

Genji nodded deeply and held his tongue. This was not so much because he was convinced, but because Yamaguchi's explanation was the kind of remark that he liked. Or at least that was how Yamaguchi remembered their exchange. Yamaguchi had in fact never turned Step's amplifier off, but even if it were a lie, Genji was very taken with the turn of phrase. Why bother to examine if a thing is true or not? Genji was happiest to be shown the seam where the bright colors of truth and fiction are interwoven. That was the kind of man Genji was.

Genji, the owner of the Fukagawa Bar, Gonbei, Yasuhara and Yamaguchi all had a great deal in common with one another even when they disagreed about things.

"Truth is…" Yamaguchi started to say. Apparently he'd made up his mind: the time had come for him to explain why he had gotten everyone together.

"A little while back, there was a woman who had been on the run for fifteen years – do you remember? And how she was arrested just before the statute of limitations would have let her off the hook?"

"Oh yeah, the one who was all over the papers and the TV," promptly answered Gonbei with a nod. The incident had been heavily covered; so much so that even Genji knew the case, though he wasn't generally much interested in the news. With the help of her husband, this woman had murdered another woman and stolen all her money. She had then split from her husband to escape police detection, and spent fifteen years on the lam, moving from one place to another, before finally being caught just a few days before the statute ran out.

The newspapers, the TV and the weekly magazines had

reported it all in great detail, so it was now nationwide knowledge that the woman had undergone plastic surgery and had kept moving from one town to another.

"You have to hand it to her though. She did well to stay uncaught for fifteen years like that," said Yasuhara, with a hint of admiration. They all nodded their agreement.

"She was quite a fine-looking woman."

"I don't know about that. They say she'd had so much plastic surgery that her face didn't look anything like her original appearance."

"To be that determined to get away – it's really impressive."

"But by that time she wasn't on the run for any good reason – just being on the run had become an end in itself."

"For all we know, it could have been a game for her, you know, to keep running till the statute ran out."

"But, what bothers me..." Yamaguchi, seeing that everybody had been able to have their little say, spoke emphatically, feelingly. "What bothers me is that it's just not possible for a person to live their life and be completely anonymous. After all, just in the course of everyday life, an adult will end up being in daily contact with about sixty other people."

"Sixty?"

"Yes. There's the janitor of the building, the person who delivers the dry cleaning, the man who collects money for newspaper subscriptions; there's the staff at the convenience store, the guard at the ticket barrier in the station, then the neighbors, and the kids of the neighbors... Reckon it up like that, and you'll see that you end up having some sort of involvement with about sixty people."

"In other words, one hundred and twenty eyeballs are gazing upon you," declared Genji, with a poetic lilt. "Meaning that if you suddenly turn up in a new town, it's basically impossible to dodge one hundred and twenty eyeballs and live without being noticed."

"But Yamaguchi," said Gonbei, who had nodded once before tilting his head inquiringly to one side, "why did you bring up this topic?"

"Well, I suppose someone among those sixty people in contact with that woman must have realized that she was a bit suspect. I mean, she got caught in the end because someone from the bar she used to go to called in the police."

"What are you trying to say? That bar owners are informers by nature?" said the owner of the Fukagawa Bar looking sulky.

"No, no. I know that you aren't the kind of person who'd do something like that. Here I think the opposite thing might happen."

"Opposite?"

"Let's say that a suspicious woman like that strayed into your Fukagawa Bar here. What would you do – give her shelter or help her escape?"

"Well, I suppose it would depend if that suspicious woman was a looker or not," replied the bar owner scratching behind his ear with embarrassment.

"Women like that are always stunning – at least they are in the theater," muttered Genji, gazing off into the middle distance.

"Very true. So ratting on the lovely lady wouldn't make for good theater – or good anything. But surely, Gen, that is the difference between play-acting and reality?"

"Gonbei, you're just a youngster. Why do you insist on holding forth like a man of the world? Here in the Fukagawa district, there is no border between acting and reality. Fukagawa, my friend, is an oasis in the metropolis called Tokyo."

"An oasis! What a clever thing to say, Gen."

"Look, even *I* know what 'oasis' means. For me, the little world of Fukagawa here is an oasis in the urban desert of human feeling."

"I have my doubts about that," interrupted Yamaguchi, as if standing in for Gonbei.

"You doubt it? You doubt the human warmth of our Fukagawa district?"

"Listen, people go on about the warm heart of the people in Tokyo's *shitamachi*, but in fact it's got a terribly conservative side to it. Let's say a suspicious woman was living in a *shitamachi* district. I think that the residents would get together like a bunch of vigilantes and drive her out in no time. Can you deny that?"

"No, I can't." Gen nodded his agreement, biting his lower lip.

"The idea of the 'Tokyo desert' is all about people's feelings drying up and withering away. Personally though, I think that not bothering about other people can sometimes end up being a sort of kindness."

"Yes, exactly. If a criminal goes into hiding in Tokyo, then the place they're going to be hardest to find isn't the *shitamachi* with its strong sense of community, but the 'Tokyo desert' parts of town where people's humanity has gotten diluted."

"When you two get talking, I sometimes find it quite hard to follow," said Genji to Yamaguchi and Gonbei. "What was that bit about criminals being hard to find if they're in hiding in Tokyo?"

Genji looked irritated as he struck a match. No sooner did the flame flare up than he shook it out in mid-air and turned impetuously towards Gonbei.

"So what you're saying is this: Because everyone shares the same narrow set of values out in the provincial cities, it's easy to tell who's suspicious and who's respectable. So, if a criminal goes to a place like that they'll be reported and arrested in no time at all, right? But because the people who live here in the big city have much more diverse values, the dividing line between suspicious and non-suspicious people is much less clean-cut. On top of that, since most Tokyoites live their lives without any particular interest in their next-door neighbors, they certainly have no reason to be interested in complete strangers. Living under these terms, they don't interfere in each other's lives. As a result, the big city is comfortable for oddballs and misfits to live in, making it a kind, sympathetic space. That was the conclusion, wasn't it?"

"Right. The fact that people's human side has gotten weaker ends up being a sort of kindness in itself."

"So as long as a suspicious person is in hiding here in Tokyo, they're safe. Anyway, when you start talking about 'suspicious persons,' everyone in the big city is a little shifty."

"Never heard a truer word. Look around you, and there's no such thing as a 'normal person.'" Riding on Gonbei's slipstream, Genji delivered this speech with great theatricality, staring at them all as he did so.

"If you ask me, Gen is the most suspicious person I know," said the master of the Fukagawa. Genji couldn't stop himself from shrinking in embarrassment and a laugh ran round the group.

"But I still don't understand what Yamaguchi really wants with us," said Gonbei after the laughter had died out. He folded his arms across his chest in the same position as earlier. Time seemed to have been rewound a few minutes, and everyone was once again looking intently at Yamaguchi.

"Well, you could say that the woman – the one who got the mass media into such a frenzy – made a mistake when she decided to run off to the provinces."

"If I remember right, just before the statute of limitations ran out on her they offered a reward of some kind, didn't they?" asked Yasuhara, looking over at the owner of the Fukagawa as if seeking his agreement.

"That's right, yes – there was definitely a reward."

"Well, that only makes the act of informing even more despicable."

"I wonder if the bunch who ratted on her out split the reward between them?"

"That's blood money. I wonder what they'll spend it on?" Genji delivered himself of another theatrical line, then crossed his arms and looked thoughtful. There was an old poster for a popular drama on the wall beside him. The hero was gazing off into space. His expression and Genji's were identical.

"Just hold on," said Yamaguchi forcefully. He wanted to bring the discussion he had started back to its starting point before it got completely lost in digressions.

" I don't think you can say that here in Fukagawa we don't have snitches like the ones who turned that woman in to the police. You can't say that we don't have that sort of vigilante attitude here too."

"I know what you mean. I sometimes wonder what's become of the warmth and kindness of the old Fukagawa."

"No, I disagree. Fukagawa is definitely an oasis in the Tokyo desert," said Genji becoming suddenly serious.

"You're right," declared Gonbei loudly in counterpoint to Genji. "At least we regulars of the Fukagawa Bar are a special breed – a Fukagawa within Fukagawa."

"All right then, how would we act if a suspicious woman like that appeared here in front of us?" Yamaguchi had deliberately posed the question in a low voice and the atmosphere became suddenly and strangely tense.

"When you use the phrase 'a woman like that,' have you got anyone in particular in mind?" asked Genji, keeping his voice low to correspond with the way Yamaguchi had spoken. At this point, Gonbei crossed his arms with exaggerated emphasis and looked at Yamaguchi with a provocative "well what have you got to say to that?" expression. Yamaguchi could not prevent his lips curling up into a smile: the two of them looked so theatrical, like the classic confrontation between an old father and a rebellious son. Yasuhara cocked his head as though unable to imagine what Yamaguchi's reply might be, while the owner began studiously wiping the glasses lined up on the bar.

It felt as though time in the Fukagawa Bar had suddenly begun to flow more slowly. There was more than an hour to go until opening time at five o'clock, but inside the bar the main door was shut tight, making it as dark as in business hours. It was difficult to guess what time it was and an atmosphere of mystery enveloped them all.

"Yamaguchi, I think you're trying to imply that the woman, the criminal who got arrested, was a regular here," said Yasuhara.

"All I said was I wondered what we would do *if* she had come here," he said. He wore a defensive expression.

"Yamaguchi, are you telling us that you called us all here – and you know we're all busy men – just to ask our advice on an imaginary issue?"

"Oh come on, Gen, none of us are busy at all. We're all men of leisure."

"Speak for yourself! I've got a heck of a lot to do at home. There's looking after my grandson, supervising the education of my daughter-in-law..."

"Ah, here we go again. Look, we all know you live alone, Gen."

"Gonbei, you're a young man but you still insist on contradicting everything I say. Perhaps we were enemies in a previous life?"

"I'm not contradicting you. I'm just saying what's true."

"To thrust reality upon a person who is play-acting is surely the same as contradicting them?"

"Okay, okay, let's stop your little argument scene right there," interjected Yasuhara, determined to rein in the exchange between Genji and Gonbei, which looked as if it might go on a while.

"It's...er...Yumeko I wanted to talk about." Yamaguchi had finally made up his mind to speak.

"Ah, Yumeko. Yes, she's a nice girl. Don't get many like her nowadays. What is it? Has something happened to her?"

Genji looked startled as he returned Yamaguchi's gaze.

"Personally, I think she might be on the run from the police."

"You're trying to say that she's doing the old 'stay on the run till the statute runs out' act, just like the woman who put the media into such a feeding frenzy?"

"Yes, that's what I'm trying to say."

"Oh, come on. That's impossible."

"I'm sure the owner and the regulars of the bar that the woman who got arrested went to thought exactly the same thing."

"No, but Yumeko's not like that. She's not that kind of woman. Right, Gonbei?"

"She's certainly a good-looking woman, but I'm not able to say if Yamaguchi's right or not."

"You're not able to say? Have you got eyes in your head? I can't believe that you suspect her of something like that. You agree with me, Yasuhara, don't you?"

"Well, yes, I agree it's hard to believe it of her. But when someone suggests it – you know, it's not completely..."

"Oh, so you can't see what's in front of your nose either. Okay, you run this bar, so I'm sure you've got a knack for seeing what people are really like. Myself, I think that with Yumeko the whole crime thing is completely impossible. What about you?"

"Uh..."

"So even you have your doubts... Ah, the old human kindness of Fukagawa is no more," declaimed Genji, mimicking the expression and gestures of a well-known actor.

Everybody really likes her, thought Yamaguchi to himself

again as he inspected the gloom on the good-natured faces of the Fukagawa regulars.

Yumeko was a woman who had first appeared out of the blue just a half-year or so ago, and popped in from time to time thereafter. She was somewhere in her late thirties or early forties, and was quite petite with a good figure. Although no beauty queen, her features were regular and her complexion was fine-grained and pale. Her laugh was a little hoarse and seemed to squeeze its way out of her, accompanied by its own peculiar shadow. This piqued the interest of the regulars at the Fukagawa Bar.

Yumeko said that she sold insurance, but she had never approached any of the customers of the bar. And though she said she lived nearby, her everyday activities left no trace. Her mysterious existence was further enhanced by her name, which was written with the characters for "child of dreams." All this made her very alluring, and the regulars had come to regard her as a sort of Virgin Mary-like cult figure.

"Who'll be the first to take the plunge and ask her out?" teased Genji (who had retired from that particular race early on), nudging the other regulars and glancing over at Yumeko with a mischievous look in his eyes. It had only been a few days ago. Genji seemed to be suspicious of Yamaguchi, and in an effort to discourage him, warned him: "Don't use any dirty tricks like making her listen to jazz or anything like that."

"You shouldn't make jokes like that. Jazz is jazz and women are women," retorted Yamaguchi, thinking at the same time that it sounded like a good strategy. Undoubtedly, there was something arousing about Yumeko. She gave you a sentimental kind of feeling as if you'd met her somewhere before; but she also made you feel she was a new species of woman, a type you had never yet encountered. It was the blending of these elements that created a single, powerful mystery.

"Maybe a certain mystery only makes a woman more attractive," Yamaguchi muttered to himself. He imagined himself walking with Yumeko, and smiled to himself. Then he hurriedly wiped the dreamy expression off his face.

Of this bunch, the only person who could really get close to Yumeko is me... Yamaguchi had a sort of self-confidence. Genji, he reckoned, was probably too old for anything other than a platonic relationship. As for Yasuhara, apart from coming for the odd drink at the Fukagawa, he was the type of person who sat stock-still in his shop and gazed off into space. That half-assed business of his was not busy, so work afforded him little reason to go out. When his wife came in with green tea he would pose as a tragic figure, sighing as he contemplated how the old fastidiousness that demanded a tailor-made suit that last for life was dying out in a new age that preferred Italian fashion and cheap ready-to-wear business suits.

Someone like that was unlikely to feel any interest in Yumeko, thought Yamaguchi, looking at Yasuhara with a feeling made up half of pity and half of relief.

Gonbei, whatever the impression he may have given people, was actually a workaholic. He also made a clear distinction between his passion for Fukagawa and his real life. Like Genji, Gonbei also liked to play games in the gray area between acting and reality. But like a student whose training is not quite complete, he had not quite mastered the art, which occasionally made him seem something of a sage. Perhaps it was due to the regulars at Fukagawa, all older than he was, accepting him into their circle that he had a certain aura of humility, which lent him an old-fashioned charm. This in turn led Genji to tease Gonbei affectionately by laying down the law to him about all sorts of things.

But Gonbei was also still unable to understand the charm of the mystery surrounding Yumeko, thought Yamaguchi.

No, more than Gonbei, the owner of Fukagawa Bar was the rival Yamaguchi had to watch out for most. The owner's past was a mystery and that gave him something in common with Yumeko. *Like follows like.* Yamaguchi had heard that proverb somewhere, and the owner and Yumeko certainly had the necessary elements to hit it off. The owner's wife had died three years ago, so perhaps the time had come for him to make a move of some sort. The owner, who had seen all kinds of people from behind the bar, seemed like the sort of man Yumeko might well be drawn to. If you thought about it like that, then the master was without doubt his most formidable rival.

Unfortunately though the master was developing diabetes and was recently finding it hard to stay the course, whatever he did. The time he had spent on the other side of the counter contemplating other people's lives was certainly a weapon in his favor, but you couldn't help feeling that over the years he'd gotten into the habit of looking at things from a safe distance. Yamaguchi comforted himself with the thought that the owner probably couldn't get really energetic about anything.

Maybe I should I invite her over to my café sometime.

This thought had often occurred to Yamaguchi when he watched Yumeko come in the Fukagawa Bar, invariably alone, sit down at the corner of the bar, and then join in the general conversation of the regulars completely naturally. Genji may have made fun of the idea, but jazz, he reasoned, would certainly work to his advantage... Thus Yamaguchi encouraged himself in his attempts to break through Yumeko's veil of mystery.

Five days ago, Yumeko had come to Step. It was empty and Yamaguchi had been absent-mindedly reading the horse racing paper while playing a piece of jazz he liked to listen to when on his own. He raised his eyes – and there right in front of him was Yumeko's face. He smiled and stood up. The scenario he had schemed and fretted about so much had become a simple reality before his eyes: he felt it to be a true jazz moment.

"I can't explain it, but when I listen to old jazz I feel somehow refreshed," Yumeko had suddenly said in her famously husky voice, sipping her coffee. To Yamaguchi, Yumeko's profile here in the jazz-café seemed to be that of a completely different person to when she was sitting at the bar of the Fukagawa. There was something determined about the outline of her face, which brought the word "mysterious" into Yamaguchi's mind.

"I wonder why listening to jazz makes you feel refreshed?"

"Because jazz is the best music to forget to."

"Ah."

"That's why I go to jazz-cafés when I feel unhappy."

"When you feel unhappy…"

"You don't think so, Mr Yamaguchi?"

"Well for me, listening to jazz is part of my job."

"So what do you do when you feel down?"

"I've got some tracks that help me feel better."

"Such as?"

"Such as the piece I had on when you came in just now."

"That? Who was it?"

"It was Thad Jones. It's called 'A Child is Born.'"

"So that's the track you listen to when you're feeling down."

"When I listen to it – how can I put it – I forget my crimes."

Yumeko was silent.

"It's not that I've actually committed any crime, but you know how sometimes you feel driven to do something really bad? The music keeps that urge down."

"Mr Yamaguchi, do you sometimes feel like committing a crime?"

"Well, yes, sometimes I do."

"Really."

Yumeko looked deep into Yamaguchi's eyes without blinking. Then she gave a brisk nod, as if she had made sure of something, and sighed to herself.

Just then two men came in and sat down at seats at the far end of the café. As he walked by, one of them ran his eyes over Yumeko. When Yamaguchi went over to take their order, they both asked for coffee, but their eyes were fixed on Yumeko. She's the kind of woman men like, thought Yamaguchi, looking at the two of them complacently.

You, my friends, are just gawping at her like that, but I am about to get very cozy with her indeed. And at the end of the day she was the one who made a move on me.

Turning this phrase over in his mind, Yamaguchi put the coffee down on the men's table. When he turned around, Yumeko was putting the money for her coffee by the cash register. Yamaguchi rushed over and handed her the change.

"Nothing beats the sound of a vacuum tube amplifier," she commented.

"Got to go already?"

"Thanks to you, my troubles have gone."

Yamaguchi was silent.

"My life is a complete lie."

"Yumeko…"

"Thanks so much."

"See you soon at the Fukagawa Bar."

Yumeko had disappeared out of the door even before Yamaguchi had finished saying goodbye. He was about to put the money she had left into the drawer, when he became aware that the two men who had been sitting at the back of the café were standing right there in front of him. His fingers were going through the motions, but his thoughts had followed Yumeko outside.

"That woman just now – was it Saito Kazuko?"

"Well it was her first time here, so I don't know her name."

"You seemed to be on very friendly terms with her."

"Did I? Well vacuum tube amps are unusual, so people tend to ask about them."

"That woman – she likes jazz too, huh."

"But she didn't look like her."

"Could be plastic surgery."

"Think I'd better follow her?"

"The fact she came to a jazz-café is proof enough."

"How much do we owe you?"

"Six hundred yen. Has she done anything?"

"If she's the one we're looking for then she's an awesome woman."

Yamaguchi said nothing.

"Get a move on with the change."

"All right, all right. Now let's see…"

Yamaguchi took the change out of the cash register and handed it to one of the men as slowly as he possibly could. As they left Step, the two of them were tutting with irritation. Yamaguchi stood rooted to the spot. The expression on his face was like the lead character in a samurai drama who has let a pickpocket get away and is wondering whether he made it or not. The phrase 'awesome woman' echoed around the jazz-café, superimposing itself on the high notes of Miles Davis' muted trumpet, reverberating in Yamaguchi's ears.

Yamaguchi's four listeners all emitted a big, simultaneous sigh. None of them were prepared to believe his story outright. It was clear from their faces that Yumeko still remained a mystery to them.

It was Gonbei who spoke first. "We still don't know if Yumeko was the woman that the two guys were looking for or not."

"No, that's the wrong way of looking at it," said Genji, eager to undermine Gonbei. "The question is: what would we do if Yumeko really was that 'awesome woman' the two men were talking about."

"I agree. And that connects to the whole 'something special about Fukagawa' business." Surprisingly, it was Yasuhara who made this remark.

"Right, what do we... I mean, she's hiding out here, a fugitive in Fukagawa, and the question is, whether we shelter her or help her to escape," said Gonbei, taking his cue from Yasuhara.

"I wonder if it's that simple?" said Yamaguchi tentatively. He felt that the conclusion was a little bit too clear-cut and convenient.

"Okay then, what's this whole thing about, Yamaguchi? Did you get us in here to ask our advice about turning Yumeko in to the police? Do that and we're no better than the people who ratted on that woman in the news." Genji's lips were twisted with annoyance.

"No, that's not why I got you to come today. First of all, we don't yet know for sure if Yumeko is that 'awesome woman' or not. I just thought that if it does come to that, then it's a pretty flimsy basis for helping her – because we think she's hot, but know nothing about her."

"How many days ago did Yumeko go to your café?" the bar owner asked Yamaguchi, his voice quiet and controlled.

"Exactly five days ago."

"And she's not been back since then?"

"No, she hasn't."

"I see."

"You're not going to tell me that she hasn't been in here for the last five days either, are you?"

"She hasn't. Not once in the last five days. Still, I suppose it's not as if she comes in here every day."

"I wonder if she's disappeared from Fukagawa..." said

Gonbei, looking anxiously towards the door of the bar. He was copying Genji, studiously playing the part of a person concealing someone the authorities are after.

"Well, whatever she did, I'm sure she had her reasons," said Yamaguchi, remembering Yumeko's air of mystery.

"Anyway," declared Genji, looking at them all in turn, "it's a fact that we're all big fans of Yumeko whether she's that 'awesome woman' or just a woman who happens to be in trouble with the law. You got us to come in today because you want us to promise that we won't contact the police or say anything to any private investigator. Am I right?"

"You're right on the mark, Gen. Very sharp."

"But if that's the reason, it means that you don't trust us, Yamaguchi. It means you thought one of us might sell Yumeko out to the police, even though we're her friends."

"It's not like that. Something like this suddenly blows up and everything gets confused. I just wanted to make sure we all see eye to eye on this one."

"I'd never have imagined Yumeko would turn up by herself at your place, Yamaguchi," interrupted Gonbei teasingly.

"Well, she said she liked jazz."

"Oh yeah. What was it? 'When she's down she likes listening to jazz.'"

"That's what she said."

"Did she really go to your place only once?" Yasuhara frowned as he eyed Yamaguchi suspiciously.

"What are you getting at? I said it was just that one time, didn't I? More importantly, I want to know if anyone in this group was intimate with Yumeko?"

Yamaguchi scrutinized the expressions on the faces of

the four like a courtroom judge. Genji was grinning, eager to be suspected. Yasuhara meanwhile spat out the words, "What is this!" and looked away. Gonbei assumed a pose of looking flustered while trying to hide a secret, but of course that was no more than weak theatrics, Genji-style. The bar owner wore a faint smile and stared right back at Yamaguchi as if to say, "Surely it's you who's the guilty party."

"Either way, we'll never see Yumeko again," announced Genji. He delivered the line like an experienced detective who knew more than he was letting on. Somehow the other four had also had the same feeling. Yamaguchi for one was sure that he would never see Yumeko ever again. The reason he had assembled the four of them in the Fukagawa Bar and told them about the events of five days before was because he wanted to bid farewell to Yumeko in proper Fukagawa style, and he wanted them all to feel as he did. But he had the impression that the master of the Fukagawa had pulled a fast one on him in his relations with Yumeko. Yamaguchi didn't say anything, but heaped his suspicions on the manager as he dried the glasses. His intuition had told him, when the owner had smiled like that a moment ago.

Even if it is true, what difference does it make?

Yamaguchi felt a laugh of self-contempt well up from deep inside. It was not an unpleasant feeling.

"So what was Yumeko for us? What did she represent?" asked Gonbei. He directed his question to Genji, eager to elicit a comment from his elders.

"A match. Yes, a match." Genji extracted a single match from the matchbox on the bar. "A match that burns with a beautiful flame for a brief moment. That is what Yumeko was for us."

"I get it. Yumeko is the burning shaft of the match and we are the strike pad on the side of the box. The two things came together, sparked, and just for a short while we were able to enjoy her flame."

"With a match, you should just look at the flame. Put it in your mouth and it's poison. The head of a match is a mixture of red phosphorus, potassium chlorate, manganese dioxide, lead dioxide, and sulfur. The strike pad on the side of the box is powdered glass, silicon and silicon dioxide. When these two meet, they make a spark. No very major sparks flew between Yumeko and us."

"Impressive, Gen. You know the constituents of a match by heart?"

"Nothing surprising about that. I've been striking matches for fifty-five years now."

"You're a veteran of spark-striking."

"That what I said earlier. A spark is in a whole different class to a stupid cigarette." As Genji said this, he slowly struck another match. It sparked and flared up more violently than usual, then became a calm, orange-tipped flicker of blue that slowly crawled up the shaft towards his fingers at the far end.

Yumeko's mysterious face appeared for an instant within the flickering flame. As Yamaguchi tried to focus his gaze, a gust of wind blew in from outside, and the flame flickered and went out.

Everyone was thinking the same thing as they turned to look at the door. It was not Yumeko. It was five o'clock, opening time, and the evening's first batch of customers had pushed open the door and were peeping inside. Now was the time when reality began in the Fukagawa Bar. With a bored look on his face, Genji flicked the blackened, half-burned matchstick into the ashtray.

One Year Later

Mariko Hayashi

Aoyama

*I*t was approaching the time of year when Tokyo's Aoyama district was at its most beautiful. The leaves on the trees in the yard of Aonan primary school were turning to russet and gold.

Eriko liked the street that led from Aoyama Boulevard down to the Nezu Art Gallery. It was a full of brand name shops – Comme des Garçons, Calvin Klein, Issey Miyake, Dolce & Gabbana – and she walked slowly, looking at the displays in the shop windows.

It still took her less than ten minutes to get to the outdoor cafe at the From First Building. She guessed that Hiroshi wouldn't be there yet. She didn't know why, but for some reason he always arrived late. Only ten or fifteen minutes, but still it annoyed Eriko terribly; she felt it showed a lack of respect.

"I bet he's always ten minutes late with you too," a friend of Hiroshi's had said to her.

Apparently being late was a childhood habit of his. Eriko, by contrast, always arrived before the agreed time. Every time she did so, she felt she had suffered a little defeat, but she just couldn't help herself. She really liked him. What else could she do?

She had first met Hiroshi three months ago. It had been at one of those group dates which are so popular now.

"It's the chance to go out with some guys from a big trading house. You'll be there, won't you?"

Eriko had felt a little turned off by the tone of her old junior college friend Minayo. She felt she was being seen as the ditsy type who runs after guys with good jobs. But Eriko worked for a small apparel company so she hardly ever got the chance to meet men from the big trading houses. And

Minayo said they were a really friendly, easygoing bunch.

"We couldn't care less what they do or who they work for," they had told Minako. "Just rustle up some nice-looking girls for us, okay?"

Although Eriko usually wore pants and a jacket, that day she put on a suit. Having been on a number of these group dates, she had learned that the men always liked girls who dressed in a slightly classy style.

There were five girls and five boys. They went out for a drink in Roppongi but things didn't really take off. Minayo had invited girls from her company as well as college classmates like Eriko, so the evening lacked the kind of team spirit necessary to make this sort of date a success. It made everyone feel even more inhibited than normal.

They moved on to karaoke, where Hiroshi made no impression at all. It was only after everyone had piled on the pressure that he reluctantly took up the mike. He sang a hit song that was surprisingly old and square.

Hiroshi Tamura was very tall. But when a man is tall and doesn't talk much either, he's awkward to have around. Hiroshi was like that: he laughed a lot at everyone else's jokes, but never contributed anything clever himself.

"Let me tell you about this guy..."

"Now that Hiroshi..."

Every so often one of his friends would say something mocking about him.

He really should try and be less of a wimp, thought Eriko. But her initial irritation had soon turned into the desire to baby him.

When he laughed he had a lovely mouth – wonderful regular teeth. He must have done some serious brushing when he was a little boy. And his hair looked soft and not at all greasy. He had done his fringe very fashionably – it was right at the limit of what a proper businessman could get away with.

In the middle of the karaoke session, Eriko pretended she needed to go to the bathroom and left the room. When she came back, she sat down beside him.

"Hiroshi, will you give me your cell phone number?"

"Sure," he said unhesitatingly and wrote his phone number on a paper napkin on the table. Actually it was the job of the man to ask for *your* phone-number, but what else could Eriko do? If you just sat there and said and did nothing then you would get nowhere. This much Eriko knew this from past experience. She knew it though she was only twenty-six years old, and she knew that it was especially true when it came to men and women.

Sometimes Eriko would just wait patiently; sometimes she would make the first move. She had a success rate of about fifty per cent in getting her man. Instead of doing nothing and whining about not having a boyfriend it was better to at least try and give up if it wasn't working out, she'd concluded.

"You're awesome," her friend Mika had said with a sigh. "I'm so afraid of getting hurt I just can't do the sort of things you do."

When Eriko heard that she felt a little queasy. Inevitably, she had been hurt many times in the course of getting the men that she liked. She knew that it was a disadvantage for the woman to be the one taking the initiative. But if you came across a man you wanted to snare, then surely it was just common sense to put your cards on the table and have a go even if you did end up getting hurt or losing out?

With Hiroshi, Eriko felt the time had come to make a move. She hadn't felt like that about a man for quite some time.

Eriko called his cell phone two days after their first meeting. She had no idea what she would do if he was cold or offhand with her, but when she said who she was, he was very easygoing.

"Yeah, the other night was fun, huh?"

That gave her confidence, and when she asked if they could meet some time soon, he said tomorrow or the day after would be fine.

"I've just finished a big project, so I'm not too busy right now. Normally it would be difficult for me to make any arrangements in advance."

Eriko managed to interpret this as a significant and lucky omen for their relationship. She made an appointment to meet Hiroshi at an outdoor café in Omotesando the following day. Sure enough, he was late on that occasion too. She had already drunk a whole bottle of Perrier when he finally turned up.

"Sorry. I was called in by my boss just as I was about to leave."

She had thought him quite nice-looking when they'd first met, but this second time she thought she liked him even more. He looked good in the regimental tie that went so well with his dark blue suit. When Eriko found a man more attractive at the second meeting than at the first, it meant she could feel secure that the man – and her feelings for him – were the real thing.

They went to an Italian restaurant in Gaienmae. It was

very popular as it was both good and cheap. Hiroshi had gone to the trouble of making a reservation. They shared a bottle of white wine. Since it was an unpretentious place, Hiroshi put a bit of beef carpaccio on Eriko's plate, telling her how good it was and that she should try it. In return, Eriko cut him off a slice of her vegetable terrine and put it on his plate. The meal started with them behaving like a pair of longtime lovers.

He may have looked slightly dorky, but nevertheless he was a trading company man and so asked her all sorts of questions.

"What kind of clothes does your company make? What's your job there exactly?"

"We're very conservative," replied Eriko, "and the clothes we make are totally ordinary. They're the sort of clothes that a secretary would choose from the wardrobe after spending a while wondering what to wear on a Monday morning. The thing is though, when the economy's bad, those sort of clothes actually sell better. I suppose you could say my job is stock management. I just tap away at the computer all day. I studied apparel design. I knew that I'd never be a top-class designer, but I always wanted to have a job creating clothes."

She went on: "I was so psyched when I found a job at an apparel firm, but actually what I do is no different from a woman in any other kind of company. But, let's not talk about me. Tell me about you. You must get to go overseas a lot, working for a trading company?"

"No, afraid not. The section I'm in is pretty un-flashy. We buy the sort of fruit and vegetables from domestic producers that used to be imported. You probably think we trading company men get sent off to New York and Paris, but that's completely wrong. We get sent off to Kenya or to remote bits of China. Then there are people like me who only get to go to Hokkaido and Yamagata."

After they'd been chatting for a while, Eriko asked the all-important question.

"Do you have a girlfriend?"

"Sure," came the casual reply. "At my age, a normal guy usually does, right?"

"I suppose so," replied Eriko, but the wine suddenly tasted bitter in her mouth. She had thought this was the start of something, but it looked as though things were going to come to an end after this one meeting.

"I'm sorry. I wouldn't have invited you out if I'd known you had a girlfriend."

"No problem. She's not in Japan right now."

It was a common enough story. The girlfriend had worked at a car manufacturer for three years after graduation. Then this year she had quit and gone to the United States to study English for a year.

"I tried to stop her going. I don't think a year is long enough to learn anything, but it seems that women all want to go anyway."

Hiroshi spoke about the suburbs of San Francisco where his girlfriend lived.

"She says it's a really beautiful place, right by a lake. And the college she goes to is really great too. She's having a ball in the world of 'Daddy Long-Legs.'"

The instant he began to talk about his girlfriend he became very talkative. In less than a quarter of an hour Eriko was able to conjure up a clear image of her.

"How can I describe her...she's a little bit different from your average girl. She's got this incredibly clear idea of what she wants to do and she'll stick with it, no matter what people think. But I suppose that's what's I find attractive about her. Her hair? Uh, it's long. She's grown it down to her shoulders. She likes to dress in a very feminine style, even though inside – mentally I mean – she's a man."

Hiroshi continued: "We've been dating since we were students. My college and the women's university she went to have traditional links. There were lots of mixer parties. I had her down as a bit pushy, but we started dating when we were in our third year. We split up for a while after I started working, then we got together again. My friends all said we were meant to be together, but I don't really think we're old enough for people to start talking about destiny or forever."

"I'm sure you make a lovely couple," said Eriko, putting down her wine glass.

Things should have ended there, but the two of them met again the week after. This time it was Hiroshi who called her. He had a couple of theater tickets and wondered if she'd like to go and see a show with him. They saw a bizarre show at the Theater Cocoon in the Bunkamura complex in Shibuya: men dressed in women's clothes performing a play that was half-kabuki, half-musical.

From time to time Hiroshi laughed out loud. Eriko felt very happy when she saw him smile. Maybe I'm in love with this man, she thought. There was nothing that made her feel so warm inside as the sight of the smiling face of a man she was in love with. She decided that she wanted to see him again, even if it was only two or three times.

After the show ended, they went to a Korean barbecue

restaurant in Nishi-Azabu. It was just a Korean restaurant, but Nishi-Azabu being the chichi area it is, jazz played in the background and there was none of the usual smoke rising from the barbecue grills.

They talked more freely about themselves than the last time they'd met.

"I was born in Tochigi Prefecture, just a little bit outside Utsunomiya," began Eriko. "It's one of those places that's neither one thing nor the other – you know, not the country but not the town either. You felt far away and close to Tokyo at the same time. If you wanted to take a day trip to Tokyo you could. And that just made you dream about Tokyo even more.

"I used to come to Tokyo every Sunday from the time I was at high school. I'd save up my pocket money and go to pop concerts or walk around Shibuya or Harajuku. The clothes I bought on those trips were special for me. They were just the sort of cheap stuff any high school girl would buy – sweaters and skirts that only cost two or three thousand yen – but when I got home I'd try them on in all sorts of combinations and do fashion shows for myself in front of the mirror.

"At the private school I went to, my classmates always used to say to me, 'Eri, you're so cool.' There are times – you know, holidays and club activities – when you can go to school wearing your own clothes, not school uniform. Everyone used to say that there was something a bit different in how I looked, even if I was only wearing jeans and a T-shirt. Some of my friends told me I should become a stylist, but I always thought that designing clothes would be the most fun thing.

"That was when I started enjoying sewing fringes onto skirts and changing the buttons on my clothes. In home economics class, I made this awesome dress. And then when it was time for me to go on to college, I said I wanted to go to school in Tokyo. My parents weren't too pleased with that idea. They thought that a girl should just go to the local college. Yeah, my parents are unbelievably old-fashioned. Nothing you can do about that though, right? They can't help it. They've been farmers since God knows when. But they were happy enough to send my brother to university in Tokyo. It was a crappy second-rate university, but since he's a boy they said it was okay. You don't get many parents who still think like that nowadays.

"But I held my ground, and in the end I got to go to a junior college in Tokyo. I only managed to get accepted by one of the places I'd found with an apparel course. I wasn't such a keen student, you know, so I was never going to be able to get into anywhere great.

"Once I got to college, I quickly realized that my dream of becoming a designer was just a crazy fantasy. People with my sort of abilities are nothing special: there are thousands of us. The people who actually get somewhere are the ones who enter all sorts of different competitions and win prizes while they're still at college. Anyway, time went by and I thought that as long as I worked for an apparel company, I'd be happy to get any kind of job. And that's how I joined the firm I'm with now. I suppose you could describe me as a regular office worker. I'm so ordinary it's pathetic – karaoke and soaps on Fuji TV are the highlights of my existence. Anyway, your turn now. Tell me more about you," Eriko finished.

"There's not much to tell compared to you," began Hiroshi, "and I'm not much good at talking about myself anyway. I was born in Kanagawa, but we moved to Suginami Ward in Tokyo soon after. When my grandparents got old, they came to live with us. What else... The elementary school I went to was a normal public school, but for junior-high my parents sent me to Komaba Toho. I was there for high school too. My parents wanted me to become a doctor, but there were so many doctors' kids in the school with me. And when I saw the way they threw money around and what their idea of a good time was, it really turned me off becoming a doctor. Then I went to Keio University, and ended up in a trading company. I suppose I never felt the burning desire to do something in particular the way you did."

After leaving the restaurant, they went to a bar in Nishi-Azabu. There was a 'Members Only' plaque on the door and Eriko hesitated.

"Don't worry, that's just for show. Just a sort of magic charm to keep weirdoes out."

Hiroshi had been to this club a couple of times before and no one had asked to see his membership card. It was not a particularly large place. At the far end of the counter a young actress who was often on TV was sitting with a couple of girlfriends. She was dressed simply in black, but that only made her profile look even more beautiful.

"Actresses – even when you see them in a place like this – they're still really gorgeous. Look at her: she's completely different from ordinary women."

"You think so?"

"Tokyo's such an amazing place. I mean, here's a

celebrity having a casual drink in a place like this. I'm sort of used to it now. Since I got my job in Aoyama I get to see celebrities from time to time and that's when I really feel, like, here I am in the real Tokyo, breathing the same air as these stars."

"You're really something," he said suddenly, putting down his glass of whiskey and looked at Eriko intently. "You have a cool way of talking about things."

"I do?"

"Most girls don't talk the way you do."

"Is it stupid?"

"No, it's not stupid at all. You express your feelings honestly."

"Must be because I'm drunk."

"But normal girls aren't honest even when they're drunk. They're more stuck-up and pretentious. If they see a celebrity, they don't get excited like you."

"Am I embarrassing to be with?"

"No way. You're cute, you're funny and I like you. At first I was a bit...freaked out."

"The more you know me, maybe the less I'll freak you out."

"I suppose so."

Hiroshi nodded. He's gorgeous, thought Eriko to herself, looking at him smile. It was a basement bar, and the light on the dark staircase leading up to the ground level was deliberately low so couples could kiss on their way out.

Eriko squeezed close to Hiroshi and her left shoulder brushed against him. As if responding to a signal, he took Eriko in his arms and kissed her. He'd initially seemed a bit nerdy for a trading company man, but his kiss was worthy of a young man from the city of her dreams.

"What shall we do now?"

He had casually cut to the heart of the matter.

"I'm easy either way."

As Eriko said this, she shut her eyes and, as any woman would at such a time, arched her body towards him.

"Well, that's a done deal then."

He kissed Eriko once more. They emerged from the staircase into a narrow back street. A taxi came towards them with its vacant sign on, just like in a movie.

"Higashi-Kitazawa," said Hiroshi Tamura with assurance. He was like an experienced actor who had played the same scene a thousand times before.

It was not that unusual for Eriko to sleep with a man she had just met. But in fact she had only done it three times.

She'd had her first sexual experience at high school in Tochigi. A common enough pattern: she was in second grade and the boy was in the year above. It happened after six months of exchanging love letters and kisses.

But once she came to Tokyo, this was no longer appropriate. Sure, girls who jump into bed with anybody are looked down on, but girls who don't are bitched about for being frigid. Perhaps not being frigid just meant being honest with yourself and trusting your own feelings.

After all, you only go out for drinks or dinner with a man because you think he's got potential. Then if you find him nice and fun to be with, it's important you go with the mood of the moment. That was the lesson Eriko had learned since coming to Tokyo.

Of course, there are plenty of men out there who are just

after your body and proposition you crudely and directly. But an important part of the wisdom of a Tokyo woman lies in being able to tell the difference between that kind of man and the kind that might really like you. And then if you go straight to bed with someone the first night you end up feeling sad and used. Eriko was only tempted if it was likely to continue. That way, even if it didn't last long, at least she got to experience a proper relationship.

That night, resting her head on his chest, she whispered to Hiroshi: "I don't want this to end here."

"Okay," he replied. Eriko wondered sadly why he had not said *No, of course not.*

"But...I..."

"I know what you mean."

She put her index finger on his lips to silence him. His lips were still hot.

"You mean you have a girlfriend, right?"

"Well...yeah, that's what I mean."

"So what's she like, your girlfriend?"

"Now isn't the best time to ask me that, is it?"

"I know that. But I want to know."

"She's just a normal kind of girl."

"That's what men always say when they're talking about their girlfriends. *She's a normal kind of person.* What's that supposed to mean anyhow?"

"Well, after leaving university she worked for a company. Then she realized that she had things she wanted to do while she was young, so she decided to study abroad for a year. You could say she's a strong-willed girl who always gets her own way."

"What high school did she go to? Which university?"

"What does that have to do with anything?"

"You tell me which university she went to, then I can get an idea of what sort of girl she is."

"She majored in English Literature at the University of the Sacred Heart. Before that she was at Toyo Eiwa all the way from elementary school up, I think."

"Uh-huh," Eriko managed to whisper before the tears welled in her eyes. So she'd been at Toyo Eiwa for her whole school career before going to the Sacred Heart. It was the typical resumé of a well-off Tokyo girl. No way could she compete with that. But she didn't want to break up with Hiroshi at this stage. Her powerful sense of inferiority would not allow her to be the kind of woman who just fades away and disappears after a single episode.

"I've got something I want to ask you," she said.

Eriko had pulled the sheet over her head so that Hiroshi Tamura wouldn't notice she was crying.

"Can we date for just one year until she comes back?"

"We're already dating."

And he hugged her through the sheet.

"See?"

Eriko felt faint with happiness. But she still had to say what had to be said.

"When your girlfriend comes back, I promise I'll walk away. Just one year is okay for me. All I ask is that you go out with me properly."

Soon afterwards Eriko realized just how demeaning these conditions were for her.

Two seasons passed. Eriko and Hiroshi went to Okinawa for three days on summer vacation. He then took a week's holiday to visit his girlfriend in San Francisco, but Eriko could hardly reproach him for it. She could not openly show how jealous she was.

After all she was the one who had begged him to let her be his substitute girlfriend just for a year. She met Hiroshi once every week and went to his place. They would watch videos, play computer games, make love. Their relationship had continued for six months now.

Eriko wished she could see some sign of anxiety in Hiroshi's face: she hoped to catch some trace of the distress of a man torn between two women. But he was always cheerful. Eriko began to suspect that the absent-minded vagueness she had felt at their first meeting wasn't the result of frankness after all. She had recently discovered just how utterly insensitive Hiroshi could be. He had a natural ability to ignore things if they weren't completely convenient for him. But Eriko didn't find herself disliking him: as a boyfriend he had his attractions. There might be a recession on, but a trading company man had a far higher salary than your average office-worker and he knew all sorts of bars and restaurants. Hiroshi was an expert in extracting pleasure from Tokyo. He made a point of checking out happening nightclubs and restaurants.

"I've been doing this since I was at university. I wasn't in the party set, but I guess I like to check out the places everyone's talking about. That's the way I am."

Eriko's dates with Hiroshi usually started on the ground floor of the Aoyama From First building. There was a funky café there. Recently lots of open-air cafes had opened on the ground floors of buildings, but this one had been around for ages. The waiters were dressed in black suits and long white aprons, exactly like the *garçons* in Paris.

The two of them wouldn't eat there, but would walk a little way to a fusion restaurant for dinner. It had white fish carpaccio and various tasty soy sauce-based dishes. If not there, then they would walk to Nishi-Azabu where there were some very popular Italian restaurants, as well as a street with all sorts of nice-looking, great-tasting Korean barbecue places and Japanese restaurants.

In the back streets, there were plenty of fashionable bars and clubs. Hiroshi was also a wine lover, so they would go to one of the newly opened wine bars and share a bottle of wine while trying different cheeses. Sometimes they would go dancing in a club in Roppongi, but Hiroshi had started saying it was too tiring for him.

"I wasn't like this when I was young. When I was at high school, I was wild. I was really into clubbing, but I just don't have the energy anymore."

Though he was only twenty-eight, he sounded like an old man. Eriko felt both happy and sad when Hiroshi talked about his past. Even when he was just a high school student he'd virtually lived in clubs in Nishi-Azabu and Roppongi, and dined in Italian restaurants. Meanwhile she'd been hanging out in family restaurants. It was a different world.

Since they'd started going out together, Eriko had started to bitterly resent her own upbringing. She didn't wish that she'd been born to a well-to-do family; she just wanted to have been born and brought up here in Tokyo. Moving to the big city as a high school student wasn't the same thing at all. She wished she'd had the kind of life where she could casually take a train and pop across town to some happening area.

The population of Tokyo is made up of people from the provinces. People say this means nobody should feel ashamed about their origins; Eriko thought so too. But after living here for four years she understood one thing clearly: people who had been born in Tokyo were quite different from her. She could never hope to acquire that subtle blend of refinement and cynicism.

Then there was the way they were naturally blasé about where they were. When Eriko walked along Omotesando, Aoyama Boulevard or Shirogane, she was always aware of being slightly nervous. She felt she was being looked down on by the boutiques and *chocolatiers* that lined both sides of the street.

"Even now I'm just a hick," whispered Eriko to herself. She worked in Aoyama, she dressed fashionably, but still she couldn't shake off this fear.

"I was like that too, but the feeling goes away after five years. Just tough it out a little more," she was told by Yoko, a slightly older friend. "You're lucky – you come from Tochigi. I was brought up in Kumamoto in Kyushu for God's sake. I came to Tokyo once on a school excursion. Okay sure, we've got clubs and bars in Kumamoto too, but the first time I went to a club in Tokyo I was trembling all over. I mean, the way people dressed, the way they danced together – it was like another planet. But take my word for it, after you've been in Tokyo for five years and gone out with five or six Tokyo men, you've nothing to be afraid of."

Yoko added that ultimately the quickest and most practical way to overcome your complex about coming from the boondocks was to marry a born-and-bred Tokyoite.

"That's what my friend told me. She married someone

from Tokyo, and boom – her legal residence switched from Kumamoto to Tokyo. That was her happy."

Eriko could not help wishing that Hiroshi would ask her to marry him. Born inside the Yamanote train loop, a graduate of Keio and working for a big trading company: he was the kind of husband that every woman dreamed of.

Just imagine how envious everyone would be if she went back to Tochigi with a husband like that on her arm. Most of her female classmates who had stayed behind were already married, but at best their husbands had a job in town administration or in the agricultural cooperative. Even the ones who were regarded as the elite of the elite were working for the local bank or as government employees for the prefectural government.

If – *if* – Hiroshi were to choose her, then Eriko would have risen higher in the world than any of her classmates.

But Eriko knew that the chances of Hiroshi asking her to marry him were zero. He had been talking about his other girlfriend quite openly and uninhibitedly for some time now. Hiroshi said she was due to graduate in September, but instead of coming straight home she was going to visit Boston and New York with a friend first. This meant that she would be back later than expected, probably towards the end of October. Eriko took this as a warning that her time was almost up.

"Can I ask you a question?"

"Yeah, sure."

"Why are you going out with me when you already have a proper girlfriend?"

"That's just the way things are. What can I do about it?"

Hiroshi looked a bit dazed. His blankly innocent

expression caused Eriko great pain.

"When I first saw you, I thought wow, she's hot, she's definitely my type. And when we started talking it was fun and then..."

"And then – what?"

"I guess I just felt lonely, with my girlfriend in the States."

"How can you say that?" A thin, high-pitched scream came from Eriko's throat. "I'm just a substitute for you huh? Just someone to fool around with while she's away and you're feeling sorry for yourself."

"Hey, wait a minute..."

Hiroshi pulled a face if he were going to fight back. He looked so like a child at moments like this.

"Come on, *you* were the one who said you didn't mind being a substitute, that you were happy to be my girlfriend just for one year."

"Well, maybe I did."

Eriko stood glued to the spot. She saw that her own words were being used to trap her; she was tied up, helpless. She looked again into Hiroshi's eyes. The eternal question raised its head: why did this man never seem to feel any anxiety about anything? If only he'd look the tiniest bit torn; if only a cloud would pass across his face. That would be some consolation for Eriko. But he looked serene, pure, innocent.

Eriko realized then that this man did not love her one bit. She had known it before, but had been unable to believe it. She was too afraid. The truth was that she didn't want to lose him yet.

There's still two months left, she told herself. Maybe – just maybe – she could get Hiroshi to love her in that time...

But why should things suddenly change? Why should she succeed in accomplishing something she'd failed at over the last ten months? The lame old trick of getting pregnant crossed her mind, but that sort of strategy was just a joke. Anyway, Hiroshi was remarkably careful about that side of things.

Eriko wanted to scream. Her past relationships had not always worked out. Success, she supposed, would have resulted in marriage. The panic and the sadness, the sense of being hard done by – she had experienced these feelings on countless occasions when she had been unable to get her man, or when one of them had walked out on her.

But she had never experienced a pain as sharp as this. She tried to judge things objectively, telling herself that this was the inevitable result of being so calculating. Hiroshi was not the most upper-class boyfriend she'd had: he was the *only* upper-class boyfriend she'd had. Was she that impressed with his being a Keio graduate with a job in a trading company?

These may have been important factors, but they were not the only ones. The fact that her rival was so far away was the cause of a vague feeling of frustration. Eriko had never felt even a trace of her; things like a call to his cell phone, or a hint of perfume lingering in his room, or him blurting out some favorite expression of hers. Eriko had never been able to pin down any of these things.

She stared at the calendar she'd bought at a general store in Omotesando where she liked to pick up odds and ends. It was just numbers on a white background. She liked its simplicity.

One, two, three: the numbers went up as the days went

by. When you reached thirty or thirty-one, you ripped off the page. Only two pages were left. That was what they'd agreed.

"Just while she's away in the States. Let me go out with you just till she gets back. That's enough for me."

How could she have proposed something so demeaning? But her cooler judgment told her that if she hadn't, Hiroshi Tamura would never have agreed to go out with her.

I just don't understand what his feelings for me are. You saw this a lot on the problem pages of women's magazines. Eriko had never believed it. The people who wrote in just didn't want to be told the truth: they just wanted to be told things that made them feel good.

Eriko believed that women could naturally sense how men felt about them and how much they loved them: the crucial thing was whether you could accept the reality of the "how much." Most women in relationships just ignored the issue or made things out to be better than they actually were. But Eriko was different. Given the way her relationship with Hiroshi had started, Eriko was in the position to examine it and weigh up his feelings. He did not dislike her, that at least was certain. She was able to tell from the expression on his face when he was enjoying her conversation, or when he was looking at her with affection. But there was a long way to go before those feelings metamorphosed into love.

Eriko had been very hopeful at the beginning. After all, you often heard stories of girls stealing someone else's boyfriend while they were away. Provided she met the guy regularly and took good care of him, it was common sense that the woman who was physically nearer had the advantage. Face it – Hiroshi's girlfriend had just been selfish going off to study overseas like that.

Eriko thought that the tendency of Japanese women to up and study abroad when the going got a bit tough was unhealthy. You were hardly going to master a foreign language in just one or two years. Only a tiny fraction of those people ever earned a proper overseas degree. And why on earth would anyone who had a proper job and a proper boyfriend go and do such a thing in the first place?

If it had been Eriko, she would never have gone off to the States like that, if Hiroshi had asked her not to. She would have stayed close to him as an obedient girlfriend should. But she had ignored his attempts to stop her and gone off to a faraway country just to indulge a fleeting whim. Eriko thought it completely unfair that a woman like that should retain possession of his love.

It may have been no more than jealousy, but Eriko couldn't help seeing herself as a good catch who kept drawing the short straw. She looked around as she walked along Aoyama Boulevard. Whatever people might say, Tokyo was a wonderful place. Eriko had only been to Hong Kong and Hawaii, but she was convinced Tokyo was the nicest-looking city in the world.

Beneath one of the zelkova trees that lined the street, an American hippie girl was selling wooden sculptures from Bali. Sitting next to her was a Japanese portrait artist. A little further down a cute Italian girl was selling costume jewelry. She spent a while browsing before meeting up with a friend at an Italian café. If they met around lunchtime, they'd go to the conveyor belt sushi shop, where the sushi was a hundred and twenty yen per plate. Eriko loved those *kaiten* places where the plates revolved so you could choose what you wanted.

"Those places suck," Hiroshi Tamura had frowned. "If you want decent sushi, you've got to go to a place with a proper counter."

But Eriko found something uniquely appealing in tuna and squid sushi that was just starting to dry out.

Aoyama was full of luxury brand boutiques from all over the world. Stylish people and stylish cars came and went. Eriko thought again how cold-hearted Hiroshi's girlfriend must be to have left such a fun place and abandoned her boyfriend to go off to the States. She had the arrogance of someone born and raised in the capital. If Eriko had been lucky enough to possess both a Tokyo upbringing and Hiroshi, she would have shown them more respect.

Now only a page and a half was left on the calendar.

"Heard anything from your girlfriend?" Eriko asked Hiroshi Tamura off-handedly.

"Oh, you know, she calls me from time to time..."

Was it her imagination, or did Hiroshi Tamura look a bit alarmed?

"You must be pleased when she calls you."

"I guess so..."

How could she respond? Should she say something like, *"Listen, I don't want to break up with you. Can't you see me sometimes even after she's back in Japan? Let's say you see me once for every ten times you see her. I don't want things to end like this. Please..."*

But Eriko knew that she couldn't do that. She was a little surprised at herself. She thought she had no sense of pride, but it seemed to exist somewhere deep inside of her. Their relationship had been built on a humiliating foundation – her as a stand-in for his girlfriend who was overseas, her putting up with a limited shelf life – but still her pride had not completely withered and died. Quite the contrary – in fact it had grown stronger, spreading its roots to every corner of her heart. It must have been fueled by the resentment she felt about not being able to hook Hiroshi completely, despite dating him for a whole year. Eriko did not want to demean herself more than she had already. While she was mulling over the situation, the calendar got down to the last sheet.

"Eri, isn't it?"

Eriko was in a club in Hiroo with three friends from work. There were lots of clubs like it in that area; tiny compared to a proper club, but somewhere you could still drink and dance. The place was well known for its high-class clientele. There weren't many young people. It was mostly businessmen in suits from blue-chip firms. It wasn't just couples either, but groups of men on the lookout for girls. Eriko's friends had come in the hope of being hit on by them.

No sooner were they inside, than a man in a suit had swaggered over in an overly friendly way. He stopped and spoke to "Eri." She noticed the company pin in the lapel of his jacket: it was the place where Hiroshi Tamura worked. Then she remembered that he'd been sitting next to her for quite a while at that first group date. She remembered his friendly, lively eyes. He had shown some interest in her, but he'd also talked too much and generally been a bit of a clown, so she'd given him the cold shoulder.

"It's been ages, Eri. Got time for a chat?"

As he came up to the bar where Eriko was standing, it was clear that he was pretty drunk. Her friends rolled their eyes, telegraphing her to send him packing, but she paid no attention. She didn't often get this kind of opportunity. As a temporary lover, she had never got to meet any of Hiroshi's colleagues and friends. To run into someone from that group date where she'd first met Hiroshi was a real coincidence. Eriko had to take this chance.

"So Eri, I got the impression there was a bit of a spark between you and Hiroshi that evening. Did it lead anywhere? He hasn't said anything to me, but are you dating?"

"No, we are not," said Eriko firmly. "Anyway he's got a steady girlfriend, right? He's not interested in me."

"Really?"

The man looked amazed. Eriko was taken aback in turn. Since Hiroshi's girlfriend belonged to the same social class, she had assumed that his friends must have known and accepted her. She'd assumed the girlfriend was a friend of Hiroshi Tamura's friends.

"Well, I never heard anything about him having any girlfriend. Women can't stand him, he's such a retard."

Eriko suddenly felt uneasy. Hearing that her boyfriend was a failure with women made her angrier than discovering that he was a cheat and a liar.

"But he does have a girlfriend. She went to Sacred Heart and now she's studying in America..."

"Oh, you mean Mayumi?" and he gave a little laugh. "He ran after her for years so she took pity on him and went out with him for a while. When she went to America, though..." and he moved a finger across his throat in a cutting gesture,

"...she gave him the push."

"No."

"It's true. A university friend of hers is a colleague of mine. She told me they'd stopped seeing each other years ago."

A man in a suit at a table nearby who was looking their way said something to them, but whatever he said was drowned by the intro to an up-tempo song.

"Why don't you and your friends come over and have a drink with us?"

"I'm sorry, but we're meeting some people."

"Oh...you are?"

The man (she remembered his name was Kikuchi) went off without a fuss. Eriko was left alone in the music. She was utterly confused. At the same time she felt that the whole mystery had been cleared up at a stroke.

Hiroshi had been lying.

He and his girlfriend had separated a long time ago. According to Kikuchi, she had never really been interested in him in the first place. Why then, had Hiroshi told Eriko nothing but lies? He had a girlfriend who loved him as much as he loved her; that with her in America he felt lonely; that she felt lonely too and was calling him, e-mailing him. Had he really invented the whole story? Why though – was it to keep Eriko at a distance? Was it because he'd been worried she'd become a nuisance and try to pressure him into marriage or something?

No, that wasn't it. Eriko shook her head. She couldn't believe that Hiroshi was quite so deceitful. Now she finally understood what a pathetic specimen he was.

People who went to Keio University or worked at large

trading companies could be losers too. They could feel inferior, lonely – just like her. When she looked back on it, everybody had been making fun of him that time they met at the group date. Perhaps he wasn't a very attractive man after all.

She knew that there must have been many women like her who were drawn to Hiroshi's social status. He wasn't clever enough to take advantage of girls in a purely cynical way: Eriko imagined that he simply hadn't known how to deal with her. That was why he'd invented this story of a perfect romance.

She felt sorry for him. And she felt sorry for herself, the girl who had come up from the provinces and been drawn to him. True love can't exist between two losers.

She wondered if she'd ever really loved him. She felt the spell suddenly dissolve. Eriko was the one at fault. It had been obvious but she had pretended not to know. What should she do now? Pretend she'd heard nothing and keep on seeing him the same as now? No. The time they'd agreed to break up was near. Eriko was confused. She went out onto the dance floor and her body started to move with the rhythm.

"Let's dance."

Before she knew it, a tall man in a suit had appeared before her. The pin of a blue-chip automobile company glinted on his lapel.

There was a whole reservoir of replacement Hiroshis for her to choose from. She would never be a substitute girlfriend again. No, she would get herself a substitute boyfriend. And with this thought came a wave of sadness.

The Yellow Tent on the Roof

Makoto Shiina

Ginza

*W*hen I came back from work, there was a commotion at the normally hushed end of my street. Flashes of red whirled frantically here and there in the dark night sky. I was just thinking that the air had a strange tang to it, when I saw the fire engines and police cars parked down the street. From the look of things there must have been a fire. The very same moment I guessed it must have been in the building where I lived.

Horrified, I clapped my briefcase under my arm and rushed into the chaos. Apparently the fire had been extinguished some time ago; a number of firefighters in their uniforms shouted something to each other as they nimbly rolled up a hose snaking across the road.

The apartment block I lived in was called Villa Umemoto Number 1. It was called Number 1, but there was no Number 2 or Number 3 – just this one building. The landlady's name was Umemoto and it was her apartment block. She must have chosen the name in the hope of going on to construct a second, a third, a whole series of buildings. The place itself was twenty-five years old. The houses in this part of town were squeezed up against each other higgledy-piggledy, and there were hundreds of jerry-built, two-story apartment blocks. Of these, Villa Umemoto Number 1 was by far the oldest and dirtiest.

The apartments on the west side of the second floor seemed to have burned down, and one side of the roof had almost vanished. My apartment was on the first floor on the east side. A number of people were still rushing about looking agitated. I made my way through them, and was just about to enter the building when I suddenly felt someone grab my arm.

"Hey, where do you think you're going?"

The person who had grabbed my arm was a policeman. In one hand he was holding a clipboard resembling a drawing board, and some kind of small transmitter hung from his shoulder.

"I live here, man," I replied with a certain swagger. Well, the fact that I lived here didn't necessarily mean that the policeman would back off. But as he'd grabbed my arm a bit roughly, I decided to go for a 'I damn well live here, so screw you' tone.

But the policeman failed to pick up on my hostility. "You can't go in. It's still dangerous," he intoned pompously, his face a blank.

"Is anyone hurt?" I asked.

"No reports of any serious casualties at the moment, but at the present time my superior is inside making an inspection."

"Ah, Mr. Fujii, you're safe then?"

From over my shoulder came the sound of a familiar voice. It was Mrs. Furukawa. She lived in the same building in an apartment across from mine. Aged around forty, she lived alone and no one knew exactly what she did for a living. She had a round, bulbous face like a dumpling, and I've no idea whether it was deliberate or the result of indifference, but she wore round glasses the same shape as her face.

"It's terrible, awful. My legs were shaking, really they were." Mrs. Furukawa obligingly gave me a dramatic re-enactment, knocking her knees together.

"How did it start?"

"Seems nobody knows yet. They're saying that since

it was Mr. Uchiyamada's apartment that caught fire, somebody must have forgotten to turn something off up there on the second floor."

Uchiyamada had moved in around the same time as me. He lived alone. I knew nothing about him either, and I had no idea what his job was.

"Well, thank goodness the ground floor didn't catch fire. But it's been completely wrecked by all the water that came pouring down from upstairs," said Mrs. Furukawa with a grimace.

That day's inspection ended without revealing anything about the cause of the fire. We were finally allowed back in, and I gingerly picked my way into my apartment. As Mrs. Furukawa had said to me outside, the place had been drenched with water and was a complete write-off. The building, I realized, was going to have to be demolished.

I looked around my apartment asking myself which of my possessions were most important for me in my present situation. There was a lot of pitiful-looking junk, but I couldn't see anything that I absolutely had to take with me in a crisis like this. The front covers and spines of the books standing on my desk were glistening with wetness, as were the books in the bookshelf. Inside the closet, not everything was completely soaked; some things had even managed to stay completely dry.

Cursing, I hastily dragged the dry things out, and started stuffing them in order of usefulness into a trunk that had been crammed into the back of the closet. Thankfully the water hadn't done much damage to the clothes hanging in the upper part of the closet. But I didn't have many clothes;

it was all cheap stuff I'd picked up in sales or worn-out, threadbare old things.

The futon jammed into the bottom half of the closet was unusable, but I consoled myself with the thought that I was lucky everything hadn't gone up in smoke. I pulled out anything that struck me as potentially useful, and stuffed the things one on top of the other into the trunk and a couple of empty cardboard boxes.

The overall situation convinced me I should give up the idea of living here ever again. The month was already half over and I had paid a full month's rent. I could stay here for another ten days, but to insist on my right to do so didn't seem the correct thing to do now. The important thing was to find a place where I could stay the night. I pulled the trunk and the two bulging cardboard boxes into the middle of the room and pondered what to do next.

Suddenly I heard the sound of someone running along the corridor outside my room yelling shrilly. It sounded like Old Lady Umemoto's voice. She was obviously very angry and was cursing with great energy. A number of men clomped after her, perhaps in pursuit. They all still had their shoes on. This made me realize that I had politely taken off my shoes and socks and rolled my pants up before coming in. This was still my place: waterlogged it may be, but nevertheless I was not prepared to come in wearing my outdoor shoes.

"Of course I didn't start the fire! Why the hell should I want to burn down my own damn building?" shouted old Mrs. Umemoto furiously.

So, there was an arson theory. I had conflicting feelings as I gazed at the water stain spreading over the whole ceiling.

Although the building was dilapidated, the rooms here were always fully rented out. The cheapness of the rent was obviously a factor, but there'd been trouble brewing for a while now.

What was happening was that Mrs. Umemoto, the landlady, was quite openly trying to kick out all the residents. Rumor had it that she planned to rebuild the place as a larger block of apartments – hence the need for her to get rid of the present occupants as quickly as possible without making any major insurance pay-outs. Still, accusing her of arson on that basis seemed like jumping the gun to me. More importantly I still had to find myself a place to sleep tonight, I muttered to myself as I gazed up at the ceiling.

Glancing at my watch, I saw that it was after nine. I could only think of one friend who would let me stay if I dropped in at this hour in my drowned-rat state.

Aihara's place was over in Tsukishima. To get there from Kinshicho where I lived, you only had to change buses once, but there was no way I could take the heavy trunk *and* the two cardboard boxes with me. I was stumped, when I once again bumped into Mrs. Furukawa.

Things were noisy with various people still going in and out of the building. I remembered that Mrs. Furukawa's family home was somewhere nearby. It occurred to me that if I asked her she might be able to help, so I briefly explained the difficult situation I was in. Her apartment, like mine, was uninhabitable. But she had rescued anything of importance from her waterlogged room, and had gotten her belongings together as best she could.

In the course of talking to her, I found out that her family was due to come over any minute by car. We decided that she would take my boxes with her to their place. Though we were not particularly good friends, I was acutely conscious of the goodwill that bound us as neighbors and fellow-victims of disaster. We were told that any messages for residents would be passed on, then I picked up my trunk and escaped from the din and confusion of Villa Umemoto Number 1.

On my way to the station I tried to call Aihara from a public phone next to a cigarette machine outside the Hanamura liquor store. I let the phone ring for a very long time, but Aihara appeared to be out. Well, there was nothing for it but to turn up unannounced. There were only a few passengers waiting at the bus stop in front of the station. Two buses went to Tsukishima. There had been a streetcar that ran from here into Nihombashi, but it had been replaced by a normal bus service. I was in time to catch the last but one Nihombashi bus. Dragging my trunk along, I looked like a traveler setting off for someplace far away. The bus soon arrived and I asked the sleepy-looking driver about changing for Tsukishima. The sleepy driver replied in a high-speed mumble so I had no idea what he was talking about. I paid the fare and sat down right at the back.

Come to think of it, this was the time when I'd normally have finished work and would be back in my apartment chilling out with a beer. Instead, here I was on the bus heading back to Tsukishima, which was near my office. Looking at the city as it slid past the windows, my thoughts were a blur. My things were all old and crappy, but what sort of compensation would I be paid for the stuff that had gotten soaked and ruined? What about my right to live in the apartment? What would happen to that? I'd never experienced anything like this and had no idea what was going to happen. Since I didn't have enough money to move to another apartment, I couldn't help but worry.

Still, as a single man I was free and easy. All I wanted for today was to crash at Aihara's place and get a night's good sleep.

Large tracts of Tsukishima still retained the old atmosphere of downtown Tokyo, much more so than Kinshicho where I lived. I turned at a corner I recognized and, dragging the trunk, which felt heavier and heavier with every step, finally reached Aihara's stuccoed apartment building sometime past ten o'clock. There was, thank God, a light on. I knocked. After a while I could hear the sound of someone moving about inside.

"Hey, Aihara," I shouted through the door. " It's me."

I had known Aihara since we'd been at high school together. The flimsy door opened with a click. There was something distrustful about the way he opened it; it was not thrown open with a loud bang in his usual style. Aihara stood there in the doorway. He was wearing a sweatshirt that he'd obviously pulled over his head in a hurry.

"What do you want?"

"Sorry to come by so late. I tried calling you, but there was no answer so I just came over."

"What's wrong?"

"There was a fire in my building, literally a couple of hours ago. I got back from work and well, the place wasn't burned to the ground but my room was flooded and I can't live there anymore."

"Really." Aihara's expression was hardly welcoming. "So?" he added coolly. It was only then that I realized what was going on. Aihara was not alone in his place. I'd been too busy thinking about myself to realize he must have a girl in his apartment. We were both twenty-three, so it was hardly surprising that his girlfriend should drop by.

I scrapped my original speech. "So that's the situation and now can I stay with you?" was what I'd intended to say. But there was something hard in Aihara's eyes that signaled "Don't ask me that." Aihara, however, did seem to sense that I had come round wanting to stay with him.

"I have a small favor I'd like to ask you," I said. It was an idea that had suddenly popped into my head. "Are you still doing mountain climbing?"

Aihara's expression changed at my unexpected question.

"Mountain climbing? Yeah, I still go sometimes."

"That means you've still got all the equipment, right?"

"Uh-huh."

"Good. Could you lend it to me?"

At this point, Aihara stepped down, stuck his feet into his sandals and came outside. He closed the door carefully behind him.

"Listen..." All of a sudden he was wearing a look of entreaty. He held one hand upright in front of his chest as if making a prayer.

"Don't worry. I understand."

"It's just that there's someone in there with me right now."

"I told you, I understand."

"I'm really sorry. But what do you need the

mountaineering kit for?"

"I need you to lend me a tent, a sleeping bag, that kind of thing. I don't keep my kit all neat and tidy the way you do. I just chuck mine into the closet any old how. Thing is, the water the fire brigade used to put out the fire totally soaked the closet. I got a lot of things out, but they're unusable so I shoved them in boxes and gave them to someone to take care of. It was just now that I had this idea of borrowing your tent and going on a little trip somewhere."

"Okay. Planning to go to the mountains?" This was Aihara's self-serving interpretation. "Right. I'll dig it out for you in no time. Just wait there."

Shoving my hands into my pockets, I gazed up at the night sky absent-mindedly as I waited in the outside corridor. Summer was over. The sky over Tokyo was higher and fall felt imminent. About a week earlier the tail-end of a typhoon had jumpstarted the autumn rainfronts and caused heavy rain. The whole of Tokyo felt rather damp.

Aihara finally reemerged from his room carrying his camping backpack. We had been in the same mountaineering club at high school. By nature, he was well-organized and kept his equipment in good order, unlike me. The sturdy and well-filled brand-name backpack looked the same as ever.

"Here, take the lot."

"Thanks. You're a life-saver."

With Aihara's help I managed to put on the backpack. I realized I was still wearing my suit and tie. Dressed like that, it was completely bizarre to be wearing a backpack, but what was I going to I do?

"Sorry I couldn't let you stay," Aihara said in a small

voice.

"Don't worry about it. It's not a problem. Have a good time," was what I said if not what I felt. So shouldering the backpack and dragging the big trunk with my right hand, I thumped my way down the apartment stairs.

Only ten minutes had passed since I arrived at Aihara's place, but things had not turned out at all as I'd expected. I'd ended up lugging around his big backpack on top of my own big trunk, and I still had nowhere to spend the night.

What should I do? I was stumped, but I couldn't just stand there. I started walking back in the direction I had come from. All I needed was a place where I could lie down for the night. If I got some sleep, I'd surely get some bright new ideas.

I imagined there might one of those cheap old inns for commercial travelers around somewhere, since there are plenty of old houses left in the Tsukishima area. The problem was my heavy luggage. I wanted to find a place to stay quickly so that I could unwind, but wandering around in the middle of the night with no clear destination in mind was a waste of energy. What could I do? Say I succeeded in finding one of those old inns: it would still cost me a pretty penny even if I just stayed overnight with no frills attached. It was before payday so forking out that kind of money would hit me hard.

As a last resort, I could always put my tent up in a park or some other public space. Aihara and I had climbed all sorts of mountains together so I was used to sleeping in a tent. On top of that, a city park free from gusting wind, snow or rain would be a positively pleasant experience.

That's it, I thought, I'll camp out in a park. At the time I had no idea why I'd asked Aihara to lend me his camping equipment out of the blue like that. Unconsciously I'd probably been planning to camp out all along, I thought as I walked along.

In the circumstances this was my best option. Now to find a park. I'd been to this part of town on numerous occasions before. Usually it had involved going out for a drink, having a little too much, and finishing the evening crashed out at Aihara's place. Come to think of it, I'd never really walked around the area. But wandering around aimlessly with vast amounts of baggage could hardly be considered the smartest way to look. Then again, it would seem like sour grapes if I dropped my luggage off at Aihara's place so I could look for a park with free hands. I did think about stashing the trunk and backpack in a dark spot somewhere, but night or no night, this was still the middle of Tokyo and to my surprise there was no dark spot to conceal my twin burdens. There was nothing for it: I had to sweat it and search.

I turned down some narrow streets at random. The occasional car went by, but had I wanted to ask for directions there was no one around. I finally came across one of those notice boards for neighborhood news. It was difficult to see since the glow from the streetlight fell on the back of the board. I took a lighter out of my pocket, flicked it on, and examined the map of the local area. The locations of all the different shops were written in tiny kanji characters, but there was no sign of a park.

From behind me, I heard the sound of a bicycle approaching, then stopping behind me. When I turned round, I saw it was a policeman.

"Anything the matter?" he asked, looking right at me. He was directly under the street light, so I could see his expression perfectly. His tone was polite, but the suspicion was there on his face. I thought about asking him if there was a park nearby, but it was obvious that if I asked him about a park dressed in these clothes and carrying this luggage, it would only make him more suspicious.

"I'm trying to find a friend's house."

"I see. Do you know the address?"

"No, it's okay. And I came all this way too..." was my mumbled reply. The policeman subjected me to renewed scrutiny. My baggage made me look like a vacationer, but I was wearing a suit and tie. The policeman appeared to be weighing me up me from all angles before concluding that I might be an oddball, but I was probably not a thief.

"So you won't be going to your friend's place then?" he said in a friendly tone.

"No, I won't be going after all." As I casually put my lighter back in my pocket I was reminded of the fire. It had only been an hour ago.

"Anyway, it's really okay," I declared, making it clear I wanted to bring the exchange to an end.

"Glad to hear it." The policeman turned slightly and waited, watching me as I went on my way. I had the sense he would call me back any minute and my back felt hot under his gaze.

I suppose it's only natural, I thought as I walked on. The way people are dressed and their behavior takes on a different meaning depending on where they are. Take me right now. If I looked like this near a railway station, there'd be nothing odd about me at all. But wandering around in the middle of the night in a deserted alleyway downtown – that put me straight into the 'suspicious persons' category. It wasn't a good idea to keep drifting around like this in this part of town. Besides, if I didn't make up my mind soon it would get too late. And the later it got, the more of out of place I would look.

It was then that I realized that Tsukishima was quite close to my office. The company where I worked was in Ginza 8-*chome*, within walking distance. Problem was, my shoulders had started to cramp up. So I decided to find a busy main road where I could catch a cab. The main street was still as bright as ever.

I got a taxi in no time, but when I told the driver to go to Ginza, he gave me a dirty look. The way I was kitted out, he probably expected me to ask for Tokyo Station or the airport, and from Tsukishima to Ginza takes under ten minutes on foot. The driver was in a sulk; he didn't say a word as I directed him through the one-way streets to the back door of my office. He didn't say a word either when I paid him and got out with my two large pieces of baggage.

My company was in one of the many buildings that run along the Ginza main drag. It's a so-called 'mixed commercial building' with different businesses on every floor; a café on the first, a restaurant on the second and a variety of small businesses from the third floor up. My company was on the fifth floor. Now I was back at the place I had left just a few hours ago.

Since the door was locked I couldn't get into the building. But I had secretly prepared a strategy of my own. I knew the building well: beside the backdoor was a fire escape which I climbed up to reach the roof. On the second floor, there was a grille with a small gate to keep out intruders. It was easy for me to climb over this and open the door from the inside. I rather liked the roof, and would often take the elevator from the fifth up to the eighth floor and look at the view from the top of the building, my mind a pleasant blank.

You could see the water of Tokyo Bay from the roof; and on a clear day you could see the mountains over at Tanzawa. This meant that although you were slap-bang in the middle of Tokyo, at the same time you could enjoy the luxury of contemplating the sea and the mountains. I shut the iron grille of the second floor gate behind me, caught my breath and then lugged my stuff up to the roof, one piece at a time. Somehow I felt like I was climbing a mountain.

How many years ago was it that I had last gone mountain climbing with Aihara? I couldn't remember exactly. I suppose the last trip we'd done had been a winter climb of Yasugatake, our old favorite. We were always telling each other that we must go soon, but since we'd started working we never went anywhere together, though it looked as if Aihara occasionally made solo trips to nearby mountains.

I emerged onto the rooftop and felt suddenly calm. But what was I actually planning to do up here? At this stage I hadn't formulated a strategy. I just felt that up here I'd be able to erect the tent and spend the night without exciting the suspicions of the police or passers-by.

I looked around the roof. I could put up my tent

anywhere I wanted. The only problem was that the people who worked in the building came up here quite a lot. Worse, there was a real possibility that the janitor might come up morning and evening as part of his routine inspection of the premises.

It was at this point that a little tower at the edge of the roof caught my eye. A small structure, it contained the water tank and other equipment. It was a rooftop upon a rooftop. There was a metal ladder welded to it. In fact, I had climbed up there a few times.

That's the place, I told myself. I heaved the two bags onto the tower without too much trouble. The backpack was easy, but it was hard-going dragging the trunk with one hand while pulling myself up the ladder with the other, torso half-swiveled round. I was panting pretty hard after I'd gotten my stuff up there.

The top of the tower had an area of about four-and-a-half *tatami* mats. In other words, it was about the same size as my apartment over at the burned-out Umemoto Villa Number 1. A fence about twenty centimeters high ran around the straight edges of the roof and served as a sort of safety barrier.

The first thing I did was to take off my jacket so I was in my shirtsleeves. I undid the strap on Aihara's backpack and pulled everything out. There was a tent, a sleeping bag and camper-style eating utensils all packed up neatly in Aihara's signature style. I unfolded the familiar yellow tent. It was an old-fashioned tent of a type that had been popular over ten years ago, but it was trusty and reliable and had come through many a blizzard. It was the kind with twin crosswise poles that give the tent its shape and support.

There was about one *tatami* mat's worth of space inside. I put down a sleeping pad and unrolled the feather sleeping bag.

It was a tranquil and windless evening, though not clear; the sky was covered in an even blanket of cloud. If I climbed into the tent my weight would stop it being blown away. But from force of habit I knew I wouldn't settle down until I'd secured the guy ropes at all four corners.

Looking around the tower, I couldn't see any jutting object to tie them to. This is a problem you come across on mountains too, but all you have to do is find a substitute. Most often you hammer tent pegs into the ground, and if that's not possible then you find some heavy rocks to attach the guy ropes to. Everything on the tower was made of concrete, so hammering in tent pegs was not an option. The only solution was to tie the guys to something heavy.

I climbed back down to the main roof and cast around for something to use as a weight. In one corner there was a pile of rotting old building materials and construction equipment. Amongst the mess were a couple of concrete blocks. They would do the trick, but I still needed two more weights. I found a sort of rusty pole with teeth on it. I had no idea what it was for, but it was about the same weight as the blocks. A broken steel pipe chair served as my last weight. This was enough for me to secure the tent well enough.

Now that the tent was securely in place I started to look for the headlamp. The ever-ready Aihara had scrupulously included an extra battery so the lamp was good and bright. My one night's lodging was ready, albeit cobbled together from stopgap measures.

I was thirsty. It occurred to me that I'd had nothing to drink since leaving work. Finding a water supply was a matter of necessity. Climbing down again to the roof I looked for a faucet. Unfortunately my search was in vain. No sooner had I become aware of my desire for a drink than my thirst seemed to intensify. Returning to the tower, I scrabbled around in the backpack, and was happy to turn up one of those canvas water carriers often used by campers. I used to have one of them myself, but I hadn't taken proper care of it and it had gotten moldy a long time ago. Water carrier in hand, I took the fire escape down to ground level. I had a vague recollection that there was a restaurant in the building beside ours, and I was fairly certain there was an outside faucet. If I was wrong, then buying a can of tea from a vending machine would do the trick. In the morning though I'd want to wash my face, so being without water would be inconvenient.

The faucet was set back from the street in the doorway of the staff entrance. Beside it stood a pair of upended rubber boots. I rinsed the inside of the water carrier and filled it up. It had a zippered lid to make it easy to carry. Now that I had secured a supply of water for myself I finally felt a sense of calm. I had rolled up my sleeves and was washing my face, when I suddenly heard footsteps. I quickly turned off the faucet. If it was the police or a night patrolman, I was in big trouble. Whoever they were, they must have heard the sound of water. I squatted down next to the faucet and waited for them to come. If it was a policeman then everything was over.

A man appeared. He walked at a slow, stolid pace and held a number of cardboard boxes folded flat under one arm – probably a tramp. He couldn't have cared less about the water that had been gushing out so lustily until a moment ago, and he lumbered slowly on by.

Ginza was strict about keeping homeless people out, but late at night quite a number came out on the prowl, foraging through the trash cans of backstreet restaurants. I never paid much attention to them before, but now I felt an affinity for them. Still, I took care to wait until he was out of sight before going back up the fire escape.

And so, quite by chance, my strange existence began. I thought I'd crash there just for that one night; but after waking in the tent, going down to the office and putting up with the hassle of a day's work, I just wasn't up to going out hunting someplace else to live. Emotionally, I was very anxious to find myself a place to crash; but even if I did find a place, then I'd just be forced to fold up my tent on top of the tower and pack it away. After a full day's work, the idea of performing this task seemed like one big hassle.

After finishing work, I went back up onto the roof and I felt a sense of relief when I got back to my tent on top of the water tower. Of course at first I was rather worried, but people came onto the roof far less than I had expected. Still, in the course of the first week I had a number of alarming experiences.

On one occasion, I had finished my preparations and was about to climb down from the tower to the roof to go to work, when the door suddenly opened and a man I couldn't remember seeing before came out. He was in shirtsleeves, and the way he moved radiated self-confidence. Going to the center of the roof, he turned to the west and drew himself erect. Where he was standing, if he'd turned around he would have been looking directly at the top of the yellow tent on the tower. My heart in my mouth, I cautiously watched him to see what he was doing. Still facing the western sky, he made a sudden, deep bow to an angle of forty-five degrees. He then drew himself back upright, stretched his arms out wide and clapped his hands three times. It looked as though he was praying. The ritual completed, he turned sharply on his heel and without so much as a glance at my tent on the tower-top, headed for the door. Had he been praying to some god? I told myself there were numerous small businesses in this building, and he was probably the director of one of them, asking God's help with some management problem.

On another occasion someone came up onto the roof in the middle of the night. The sound of voices made me think it was more than one person. I was sure someone had spotted my tent and reported it to the janitor, who had waited till nightfall before coming up to get me.

I was rigid with fear as I waited for the two of them to come up the ladder to the tower. The sound of their voices suddenly stopped and silence and darkness returned. I didn't hear the door that led to the rooftop closing. So the two of them had to be still up on the roof somewhere. I crawled across the tower and quietly watched them. They formed a single amorphous mass in one of the corners of the roof: it was a man and a woman locked in a tight embrace.

So that's all it was. I felt relief, but at the same time I was full of goodwill towards them and hoped they would be happy whatever difficulties were in store for them, whatever sort of relationship it was. If they had to go to the trouble of coming all the way up here, it was most likely an illicit office affair.

The other thing that made me nervous was a woman who would come up onto the roof at about the same time every morning and evening. She wore a blue-striped uniform and worked for one of the companies in the building. Physically she was small, her body undeveloped and child-like. She had her hair tied in a ponytail and wore rimless glasses. I had bumped into her once in the lobby while waiting for the elevator, but I stayed stock-still as I watched her from the tower. She would go to the farthest corner of the roof where there was a pile of building materials and cleaning equipment and crouch down there for a while. Then she would skip away. I didn't see her every time she came up, but I was quite sure that she did the same thing everyday.

These episodes apart, I was having an exceptionally pleasant time. I bought in lots of convenience food and gradually adapted to the new lifestyle of my temporary home. If you wanted to be close to work, you couldn't really get any closer than I was. My commuting expenses were zero. The more overtime I did, the more advantageous it was for me.

The company I worked for was tiny – it only had about twenty employees – and it published trade newspapers and journals. As it was a men-only institution, it was a mess, with people turning up and leaving at all hours of the day. If you did a lot of overtime one day, then you were allowed to come in late the next day. I transformed myself into a keen overtime worker. After eight o'clock you could order in meals at the company's expense: that took care of dinner.

Once every three or four days I'd go out for a drink with my colleagues. If we went to a bar in the Ginza area, then I was fine no matter how late we stayed out. But there was one difficulty. Hama, one of my older workmates, lived near to my old apartment. He'd tell me in his friendly way to pile into the taxi home with him after we'd finished our drinking. I often ended up being bundled into his taxi and going back to my old place. It wasn't an easy matter to refuse his invitation, but if I made the mistake of going with him, it took ages and cost a fortune for me to get back. I developed the counter-strategy of inventing reasons to stay behind in whichever bar we were in near the office.

And so, without noticed the passing of time, I'd been living in the tent up on the utility tower for almost three weeks.

During this period, my life in the tent steadily improved. I had taken some sheets of cardboard up to the tower and spread them out evenly on top of the groundsheet. Had my tent been standing on natural ground, things would have been better. But as it was, the cold of the concrete surface was transmitted directly to my body, which was pretty hard to bear. I took a hint from the homeless man I'd seen a few days before and used the cardboard as sheeting. I replenished my supply of water while in the office and discreetly carried it up.

It had rained several times in the course of those three weeks. Aihara's tent did have a fly sheet, but it must have been defective because it leaked. To counter this, I bought a large sheet of plastic, which I draped over the outside of the tent.

The successful installation of electric power was the most epoch-making of the advances I made. It was in fact a very simple business, as I'd found an outlet near the door leading onto the roof. I bought a long extension cord and got my electricity that way. When I returned to the tent in the evening I would plug in the cord, and then I would unplug it in the morning.

The historic result of this was the ability to use electricity at night. I found an old-style electric cooking ring and an electric kettle in a discount shop (a marvelous modern version of the 'old curiosity shop') in Shimbashi. Aihara's camp stove was all right for cooking in. I could cook myself ready-to-eat meals, brew tea and heat up *sake* in the middle of the night. It was a great leap forward in living standards.

I got hold of a desk lamp, but it was so bright it glowed through the canvas of the tent. I had no idea who – if anybody – might see the tent at night, but still it would be a disaster if someone spotted a light on top of the utility tower. I decided to make do with the headlamp.

Slowly but surely fall came on. I felt enormous contentment in my tent as I warmed my *sake* before reading a thriller, as the winds of Ginza blew about me at nightfall.

I did, however, have a couple of problems. One was my mother in my home town, calling work to ask what was going on and why the letters and parcels she'd sent to me at my apartment had been returned twice. It seemed like too much bother to tell my mother about the fire at the apartment. I'd palmed her off with some plausible enough tale about hanging out for a while at a friend's place, but how long that story would hold up I didn't know.

The other problem was that I hadn't yet told my fiancee Nanae about the fire. If I told her, I knew she'd immediately start lecturing me about how I had to find another place to live. Then I'd have to provide her with my contact details right there and then. Those, I suppose, were the rules of the mating game. But I hadn't been able to bring myself to tell Nanae that I was living in a tent on my company's rooftop. Her parents were a bit snooty, and on a few occasions had already shown disapproval of my ramshackle existence at Villa Umemoto Number 1, urging me to 'try and do a bit better than that'. I could understand their feelings up to a point: Nanae and I were engaged, so as parents it was only natural for them to want their future son-in-law to have a slightly more respectable lifestyle. That was why I just couldn't bring myself to tell Nanae about the rooftop tent.

Nanae used to call me around every three days. Previously we'd met for a date once a week, but for the last three weeks I'd managed to get away with chats on the phone. Nanae, with her woman's intuition, suspected that something about me had changed and was always moody when we spoke on the phone. I needed to meet her to patch things up. That was why I really had to find a place to live as fast as I could.

I was also worried about clearing up matters with Villa Umemoto Number 1. What was going to happen about the leftover rent that I had paid in advance? Then there was my deposit. It wasn't much, but I still wanted to get it back. My salary was low and I had no savings. Without that money I couldn't even being to think about moving.

There was always something to worry about. But once work was over and I was back in my tent on the utility tower, I felt free. Screw it, I thought, who cares anyway? And I slipped into a deep sleep.

This mood seemed to be linked to the view of Ginza I had from my rooftop at night. The building fronted the Ginza Boulevard, and when you looked down from the utilities tower, the street looked like a long valley of light. All the cars and all the people moving beneath me merged to form a luminous river. The noise that came up from this river of light sounded like roughly surging waters. Naturally enough, the light and the noise grew fainter late at night, but they never ceased completely. There I was in the very center of Ginza, looking at its landscape, listening to the sounds. It made me feel that I was living in my tent at the edge of a ravine in some vast wilderness.

I had always thought that in Tokyo it wasn't possible to see the stars in the night sky. The way I lived now, I was looking up at the sky everyday and discovered that even here you could sometimes see them very clearly indeed. It was when there was a good strong wind and the clouds were scudding across the sky. The lights on the ground emitted a powerful glow, but the darkness of the lofty sky spread out far and wide. The clouds flowed between me and the sky's depths; and I saw the stars twinkling in the gaps where the clouds broke. I had the feeling that in the whole of Tokyo I alone – me and no one else – had a complete monopoly on star-gazing. It felt great. As I drank my whiskey and looked up at the stars, I felt I wanted to go on living up here on my utility tower forever.

At times like this, I sometimes used to wonder what it would be like to bring Nanae back to my new home. I imagined it would be very romantic; we could cuddle up together in the single sleeping bag, stick our heads out of the tent flap and look at the stars above Ginza. Nanae was a bit of a coward though, so I couldn't imagine her being able to climb the ladder up to the tower without making a fuss, or spending the whole night in the tent.

It started to rain in the afternoon. Over the last few days I'd carefully been following the weather forecasts in the newspapers. Typhoon No. 18 had formed out in the East China Sea, moved up north and was now slowly and steadily coming in towards us. From early evening, the rain fell in strong intermittent bursts. Come Friday and it changed into an absolute downpour. The typhoon had stimulated the autumnal rainfront and the result was heavy rain.

In the afternoon I left the office and headed up to the roof. Since I'd secured the tarp the previous day, I didn't think I had anything to worry about, but there was no harm in making one quick check. I flung open the flap to the roof – and unexpectedly found myself face-to-face with someone on the other side. He had appeared so suddenly that I almost yelled in surprise. The man who had sprung out in front of me was wearing a blue raincoat. I knew I'd seen his face before: it was the janitor. He emitted a weird laugh. He was soaked from head to toe. What had he been doing up here on the roof?

The janitor blinked, looked me in the eye and said, "What a downpour." Perhaps there was something wrong with him, but the whites of his eyes were yellow and clouded. His eyes looked heavy and out of focus with his discolored, almost yellow ocher whites blurring into the irises. He wiped his unshaven chin with one hand and said, "This weather is really something."

"Is anything wrong?" I asked, only because I was quite unable to think of anything else to say.

"Well, people were saying they thought there was a dog up here on the roof, so I came to have a look. But there's no dog here as far as I can see."

"A dog?"

"Yes, people tell me they can hear a dog whining," said the caretaker as he took off his raincoat with a loud rustling noise.

"A dog? Sounds a bit unlikely…"

I looked out at the rain beating down on the rooftop and wondered what had brought this on. Either way, I couldn't go out onto the roof while the janitor was here. But he didn't seem in any hurry to move on. I mumbled something polite and went back down the stairs. I was stupefied by the thought that for all that talk about a dog, perhaps it was my tent that had been discovered.

The rain only got fiercer as time passed. As was my habit, I worked until it was dark and then, since it was after eight o'clock, ordered a take-out from a local restaurant.

Dinner at work was limited to two places; a soba noodle shop and a western-style restaurant. I always ordered from the soba shop because their tempura and pork cutlet rice dishes were very big. Since today was the soba shop's day off, I ordered in the breaded shrimp set from the restaurant. It came with two large deep-fried shrimp, but there wasn't much rice so annoyingly it didn't fill you up properly. The young man who delivered my food was wearing a blue raincoat like the one the janitor had been wearing earlier.

There were still a few people working in the office as I tucked into my dinner. I left a little before they did.

Shutting the office door behind me, I looked around carefully before cautiously getting into the up elevator. It took me to the eighth floor from where I had to take the stairs up to the roof. Climbing up onto the tower was no easy matter as the ever more violent wind drove the rain at me, soaking me. An umbrella would have been next to useless, so, wet as I was, I just climbed on up. The wind was shaking the tent, but nothing serious had happened and it was still there. I opened the flap which I had taken care to shut tightly, and collapsed limply inside without bothering to take off my sodden clothes.

I had experienced the rain on several occasions in the course of living up on the tower. But I couldn't help feeling a bit alarmed by this combination of rain and sharp gusts of wind. I guessed it would be okay: I was hardly going to be blown off the roof, tent and all.

I felt resigned as I took off my suit, which had gotten soaked through in a matter of seconds. There were a couple of hangers dangling from the roof of the tent and I hung my suit on one of them. I then realized that when I'd climbed up to the tower, in my haste I'd brought the electric cord with me in my briefcase. Oh well, no chance of turning on the electric cooker or the kettle tonight. Damn it! Just when I thought I could take it easy at last. But I couldn't face climbing down the ladder and getting soaked all over again.

It was early – only just past eight. I didn't feel like doing anything so I plunged deep into my sleeping bag, clasped my pillow with both hands and just lay there until I finally began to feel sleepy.

The sound overlapped with someone yelling in my dream. I can't remember exactly what happened, but the dream was made up of a series of short episodes that made me uncomfortable and irritable. I heard a cry through the wild wind and rain. In my dream the cry had come from a woman. She had been chased to the corner of the roof and was holding her hands to her face in horror as she screamed. The final fragment of the broken dream was linked to reality – somebody *was* shrieking; an extraordinarily high-pitched sound against the wind and rain. But it was not a woman.

A dog! I sat bolt upright with my upper body sticking out of the sleeping bag, unzipped the tent flap and stuck my head out into the rain. No doubt about it, the yapping of a dog was audible over the noise of the rain. I didn't know what time it was. I looked down from the tower over to the chasm between the buildings on the Ginza, but through the rain it was no more than a blurred belt of hazy light. Drowned out by the noise of the rain, the traffic sounded further away than normal. I clambered down the ladder of the tower and tried to find out where the dog's barking was coming from. It was from behind the pile of building tools and other junk in the corner of the roof.

I hesitated a little, but clearly there was only one course of action open to me. The tools seemed to have been abandoned years ago. I started to pull them aside one by one, getting nearer and nearer to the barking as I did so.

By the time I found the rain-soaked puppy (which looked like a bundle of dirty rags), I was soaked through.

So that was what it had all been about. As I cuddled the jet-black puppy, I finally understood why the woman in the blue-striped uniform had been coming up here morning and evening. I guessed that she must have found this puppy somewhere and was now secretly looking after it up here on the roof.

I put the puppy inside my jacket. A good squeeze and I could have wrung water out of him. Straightaway my shirt was waterlogged. As I was completely soaked anyway, it hardly mattered. I felt almost disappointed by the speed at which the dog calmed down and stopped barking when I put him inside my jacket. I climbed back up to the tower, taking care not to knock my midriff (where the dog was) up against the ladder.

Back inside the tent, the first thing I did was to get out of my wet clothes. I then used them to give the dog a good rubbing down. I took dry underwear out of the trunk and changed into it before wrapping up the dog in an old towel. Having now calmed down, I climbed into the sleeping bag together with the dog. We were deep into fall. I was soaked to the bone and freezing cold. It took ages before I stopped shivering.

Come morning, I found that this unlikely episode was no dream but a reality. The rain was still falling, but not as heavily as the day before. After a little initial bewilderment, I got some bread out of my bag of provisions and made a simple breakfast for the dog. I then got ready for work the same way I always did. When I started moving around in an effort to get dressed, the puppy got frisky and started nipping at the ends of my shirt sleeves and pants. Pitch-black and with perfectly round eyes, he was eager to come up and nibble my fingers. The biting never hurt at all; I enjoyed it. After all, it was just his dog-like way of having fun.

What to do with Fido here – that was the question. I was sure that the woman in the blue-striped uniform was taking care of him in secret. That meant that she was sure to come up onto the roof today to feed him or whatever. If he wasn't there, she'd get all desperate and start looking for him. But with this relentless rain, I really had no desire to put him back in the heap of junk where I'd found him. After he'd happily lapped up his bread soaked in milk, the puppy curled up on the sleeping bag and fell asleep.

Well, there was nothing I could do about it. I resigned myself to fate: what will be will be, I thought. When I opened up my umbrella and went outside, the dog followed me in something of a panic. Then, although it was raining, we took a little walk together around the edge of the tower.

Since the tent took up about half the space on the top of the tower (which was only about four-and-a-half *tatami* mats to start with), there was very little space to walk. But it was room enough for the dog to pee and poop. Even so, there was no way he'd be able him to restrain himself until I got back – he was probably going to end up doing it in the tent. The idea of the dog's pee and poop sloshing around in that little tent was unbearable, but I couldn't very well just chuck him outside in the rain.

I put the puppy back in the tent and he curled up quietly on top of the sleeping bag and settled down. I went down to work at the usual time and worked through until lunch. All the while I wanted to go up and check on the tent but I stopped myself. If I went for a look, woke the snoozing dog and he started barking, that would just lead to a new set of problems.

On Saturday work stopped at midday. So I hurriedly finished off what I was doing and went back to the tent. As I started climbing up the ladder of the tower I heard the dog beginning to whine; he seemed to realize it was me. It was no longer raining very hard, so it struck me I'd soon be able to put the dog back where I had found him. Had the woman already come up? She'd left no traces, so it was difficult to know.

Nowadays, the majority of companies take Saturdays off, but I had no idea what kind of timetable her company followed. Anyway, there was nothing I could do about it. You can see I was in my usual 'couldn't-care-less' frame of mind.

It was hardly raining at all now. Luckily the typhoon had headed off towards China and the autumnal rainfront had moved northwards. The weather in the Kanto region would improve rapidly from the evening. The dog – good for him – had done neither a pee nor a poop. I put him outside the tent and let him do whatever he wanted for a while. As it drizzled, he charged hither and thither around the small area, then did his business in more or less the same place as in the morning.

The tent had acquired an unexpectedly lively atmosphere thanks to the puppy's presence. Anything and everything in the cramped tent interested him, and he would bite and sniff around, checking out different objects. But it was the sleeping bag that he liked more than anything. I suppose it was because the sleeping bag had provided him with such comfort when he'd been reduced to a state of drowned-rat misery on the day of the storm.

The next day the weather was wonderful; the proverbial sunshine after the rain. The sky was marvelously clear in every direction, and from the top of the tower it was possible to see both the sea and the mountains. As it was a Sunday, there was not really anyone in the building, and the janitor wasn't there either.

The dog and I came down from the tower and took a morning walk. I felt so free. Having said that, we were limited to the roof as I could not take the dog down to ground level. The dog kept his distance from the pile of things he had been concealed in till recently. I supposed life in there must have been pretty rough. It had never occurred to me that walking a dog on a rooftop could be so pleasant an experience.

Still, I had plenty to do that day. After two full days of rain, the tent was of course soaked, as were my clothes and the sleeping bag. As I set to work, the dog mistakenly imagined I was playing with him and ran after me wherever I went, shooting through my legs. I had to be very careful not to tread on him. Carefully pulling everything out from inside the tent, I spread it out on the dry concrete rooftop. I put weights on the lighter things to stop them blowing away. The cardboard under the tent had absorbed so much water it was unusable. I had to get a new supply from somewhere. It was the sleeping bag that was in the worst state. I hadn't been aware of it but the underside of the down sleeping bag was waterlogged and wasn't going to dry easily. I devoted the whole day to drying my things, then had dinner with the dog.

The dog had become very attached to me and appeared to have gotten used to life in the cramped tent up on the tower. He may only have been small, but he was a quick learner. It was easy to clean up after him as he was considerate enough to always do his business in the same place. That evening I went down to ground level and bought myself three cans of chilled beer from a backstreet vending machine in Ginza 8-*chome*. Nothing tastes quite like a weekend beer with a night view of Ginza.

It occurred to me that soon it would be a month since the fire. The storm had passed and the progress of fall was palpable in the dark of the night. The wind that blew in from the sea was stronger. Thankfully, there were still plenty of stars shining directly above my head. I suppose that the stronger winds blew the smog and the pollution clean away to provide me with a wonderfully clear view. That day I could see right to the far side of Tokyo Bay. Presumably the lights twinkling on the horizon were the industrial part of Chiba Prefecture.

The city sounds of nighttime Tokyo rode the wind and danced arabesques in the sky. It was with an extraordinary sense of well-being that I gulped down my beer. At my feet the puppy was curled up contentedly. I gazed in happy vacancy at his black fur being blown to one side by the strong gusts of wind that now and then rocked the tent.

It occurred to me that I had originally planted my tent here intending just to stay a day or two. Once I had started living here however, it turned out to be unexpectedly cozy. I was thrilled to discover it could be comfortable and pleasant not just in nighttime Tokyo, but in nighttime Ginza, the very heart of the city. If I could have my way, I thought, I'd like to keep on living here like this.

There was something I had to make a decision about.

Tomorrow was a Monday so I had to decide what to do with the puppy. The woman would definitely come up here tomorrow. When she found the puppy was missing she'd be sure to get desperate and start looking for him everywhere. If he chose that moment to start whining then everything was finished. What should I do? But the beer made me feel pleasantly lightheaded and my usual irresponsible 'who cares anyway' attitude took over.

The wind was considerably stronger, but it looked as though the weather on Monday would be splendid too. The early morning wind blew off the sea and shook the tent violently. I firmly re-tied the guy-ropes at the four corners of the tent, and rearranged the baggage inside in an attempt to balance things so that the tent would not be blown away.

My things were more or less dry after being hung out to dry all the previous day; only the down sleeping bag was still heavy with wet. I'd hoped to dry it out properly the day before, but that hadn't worked so I decided to put it out to dry while I was at work. It would be a catastrophe if my sleeping bag blew away, so I placed a number of concrete blocks on it as weights. I was in two minds about what to do with the dog, but finally decided not to bring him down off the tower and to leave him up there while I went to work. The rest was fate. I made myself presentable and went down to the office.

As usual, I was the first person there. I boiled some water for tea and gobbled down some *onigiri* rice balls I'd bought the day before. No doubt about it, tea made from water boiled over gas in a teacup was nicer than tea from a plastic bottle heated up in a metal cup in the tent.

As usual the head of accounts arrived a little after me. "Early as usual, I see?" he said, just as he did every day. Before everything happened, it was the head of accounts who had always been first in to work. I laughed in non-committal agreement and began my work promptly. Nine-thirty was the official starting time for us, but the rest of the staff turned up in their own sweet time. It was usually after ten before everyone was there.

The president made a speech as he always did on the first Monday of the month. It was the same old spiel every time. "The economic environment that surrounds us is of an unprecedentedly challenging nature. That is why you must raise your game and apply yourselves whole-heartedly to your work with diligence and dispatch." This was followed by the managing director presenting a few detailed reports – and that was the morning meeting over and done with in all of fifteen minutes.

I tried hard to do some overdue work, but kept worrying about what time the woman would go up to the roof, high up there above the ceiling of my office.

It must have been just a little bit before lunch when Sayama, a colleague of mine, glanced absent-mindedly out of the window and asked me in a bored-sounding voice, "What on earth's that? A snowstorm? But why should there be snow on a sunny day like today?"

The window that Sayama was looking out of faced Ginza. Propelled by the gusting wind, snowflakes – or something like snowflakes – were dancing and swirling around on the other side of the glass. As Sayama had said, it really looked like a snowstorm.

"Huh? What the *hell* is that?"

I stared intently at the scene outside the window for a few moments. I felt as if a sudden, sharp pain had exploded in my spine. I rushed over to the window and took a careful look. It was a remarkably blue sky for snow. Countless soft flakes were wildly swirling around. I opened the window and looked up. Just as I thought, the soft flake-like things were being picked up and blown off the top of our building by the gusting wind.

"What the hell?" I muttered under my breath. I realized that the 'snowflakes' were coming from my sleeping bag on the tower on the roof. What could have happened? I looked dazedly up at the roof and the feathers falling from it, then snapped out of my daydream and charged out of the room.

My guess was a hundred per cent correct. Climbing the ladder up to the tower, my eyes were confronted by a cloud composed of countless feathers, drifting and dancing in the wind. Beneath the cloud, I saw the black, round-eyed puppy running in a happy frenzy on top of the sleeping bag, as feathers poured out from a huge gaping hole.

The Housewife and the Police Box

Chiya Fujino

Shimotakaido

1

*I*t was night and Natsumi's only daughter Mika, who should have been asleep hours ago, appeared in the living room with her curly brown hair floating about her shoulders. "Mommy," she asked shyly. "Mommy, why aren't there ever any women in police boxes?"

"What? No idea," replied Natsumi offhandedly, busy watching *Deep Impact* which she had just rented from the video store. Then, overcome with a sudden feeling of guilt, she produced a proper "concerned mom" face, paused the tape and said, "Hmm yes, I wonder why not?"

The truth was that Natsumi hadn't been aware that there weren't any women police officers stationed in police boxes: until then she'd never given it a moment's thought.

"The most important thing is for you to go to sleep. You'll be late for school otherwise."

As she came out with this cliché, Natsumi smiled at her daughter. Mika, who was wearing pajamas decorated with a monkey character, realized it would be a waste of time to ask her mother any more questions. So she looked up at her cheekily, said, "So you don't know, huh?" gave one huge theatrical yawn, and left the room with an "Okay, 'night."

"Why police boxes?" puzzled Natsumi, her hair pulled back off her high forehead with a black and white striped hair-band, lips pushed forward in a duck-like pout. But five seconds later, she had been drawn back into the movie and quickly forgot the whole conversation.

She remembered it the next day though. It was while she was doing her shopping at the market near the station that her daughter's question came back to her out of the blue. *Why aren't there ever any women in police boxes?* The question just popped into her mind, so it seemed natural to ask the young woman from the delicatessen. She didn't seem at all surprised. "Come to think of it," she replied cheerfully, "you're right. You don't see any women, do you?" Then lowering her voice slightly: "What happened? Has someone stolen your panties from the washing line?"

"No, no," replied Natsumi, shaking her head. "It's something my daughter asked me."

"Oh, Little Bebe asked you?"

For some mysterious reason, the chatty woman at the delicatessen always referred to Mika as "Little Bebe." Her young husband, who was standing next to her filling a container with macaroni salad, joined in cheerfully "Ah, Little Bebe – she's already going to elementary school, right? Was this her assignment?"

"What grade is she?"

"Second grade."

"Really."

The young couple at the delicatessen in their matching white aprons had known Mika from kindergarten age.

Natsumi bought some scrumptious boiled beans and dried *mirin*-seasoned sardines, along with the macaroni salad. She stuffed everything into her big straw shopping basket and left the narrow arcade where the market was.

The covered market merged directly with the main shopping street. Right in front of this stood the two-floor Keio Line station building. The train tracks lay there with a dull gleam. Beyond these ran the two-car Setagaya Line train. There was only one Shimo-Takaido station, but the two train lines had separate platforms and separate ticket barriers. One line went to Shinjuku, the other to Sangenjaya, and the tracks quickly diverged into a V.

Natsumi had last used a train more than five months ago, so it didn't matter much to her what lines they were and where they went. As long as they weren't bullet trains or TGVs, which would be too noisy, then that was fine with her.

Natsumi very seldom set foot in the station building. Recently it had been to see off her husband, who had been transferred out of Tokyo and was now living alone near his work, or to visit the bookshop on the second floor. On that day, her husband wasn't with her and she didn't need anything from the bookshop either, so she walked past the station and went to buy a couple of giant cream cakes from a bakery chain. Since the shop assistant went to the trouble of asking, Natsumi got her to pack thirty minutes' worth of dry ice. Then she walked over the grade crossing and returned *Deep Impact* and two other movies to the video store without renting any new ones.

Why had Mika asked that question?

Coming out of the video store, Natsumi started to walk in the opposite direction away from the grade crossing. She was planning to go home by a roundabout route; but perhaps she had another, subconscious purpose. Until last month Mika had been obsessed with Crione, a mysterious deep sea creature. Now why on earth had she suddenly switched to police boxes? After all, she's a girl, not a boy... After a while, Natsumi came to a halt in front of a police box. It was a little past the rental video shop on a corner just after the elementary school front gates.

If you looked carefully, you could see the police box

had two floors. Two floors, Natsumi duly noted with half-hearted interest. Until this point in her life, she had never felt a flicker of interest in police boxes. The shrill sound of children could be heard from the elementary school. Its fence was made of large children's drawings slotted into metal frames. Perhaps it was break time right now? Or maybe school discipline had just completely fallen to pieces? This wasn't the school that Mika went to. This was a Setagaya Ward school, but the apartment where Natsumi and Mika lived was across and along the Koshukaido road a little, so her school was in Suginami Ward instead.

In the police box (she supposed that in the same way as Mika's school it didn't cover the neighborhood where her apartment building was) there were two policemen wearing navy blue caps and blue long-sleeved shirts. It was a very small sample so it was hardly reliable, but just as Mika had said, they were both men. Perhaps because of the impact of their uniforms, they looked like identical twins. Both of them were solidly built.

Apart from the two policemen, the only other thing in the four-and-a-half *tatami* mat area of the concrete building was a big bulky steel desk. There was no sign of any other furniture or decoration. A cuddly toy of Pin-Pon, the orange police mascot, was plunked on the window ledge facing outwards, smiling at the world. There were a number of fold-up metal chairs and silver shields like those used by the riot squad propped up against the gray wall. On it was taped a wanted poster with pictures, probably of people connected to the Aum Supreme Truth cult.

One of the two young policemen was sitting at the desk. What could he be doing? He had the telephone receiver glued to his ear but wasn't saying a word. The other one stood behind him flipping through a thick file. From time to time he held a page open and looked down with an intensely serious expression. While Natsumi was observing him, he suddenly lifted his head. Their eyes met for a second through the plate glass window, which reminded her of a deejay booth.

Not wanting the bother of being questioned by them, Natsumi brought her hand slowly up to her chin, tilted her head a little to one side, then stared down at the shopping in her basket. Perfect! The idea was to look like a housewife who had stopped in her tracks and was anxiously wondering if she'd forgotten to buy something for dinner.

2

These days Natsumi didn't take the train. It wasn't that she didn't need to; it was simply that she couldn't. For many years now she hadn't been too good with any form of transport, but trains were worse than anything.

She guessed that the first time she'd felt this train-phobia was back when she was commuting to her private high school in Tokyo. It had been rush hour, and the train was crowded with children on their way to school. Suddenly she was attacked by overpowering nausea and dizziness.

It was probably the result of a problem with her inner ear, which was a bit weak. She was sweating with anxiety, but would probably have been able to tough it out for a short time. But unluckily the train had then come to a stop between stations.

"There has been a suicide involving the train in front of us. We have to wait here a while," a bored-sounding voice announced, giving more information than was strictly necessary. So Natsumi started imagining the bits and pieces of the crushed body of the person who'd been run over by the train. She couldn't stop herself, and threw up everything she'd eaten at breakfast over the blue-suited back of some salaryman she'd never seen before in her life.

Warm goo fell in dribs and drabs out of her mouth. She felt like she'd turned into one of those large water-spewing lion-face taps you see in public baths. She couldn't remember much except hearing a confusion of voices, but she wasn't sure if they were screams, jeers or cheers. When she came to, she was lying down in the office of a station she didn't recognize.

"Are you all right? Are you feeling okay?"

An old railway employee, the spitting image of the actor Ken Takakura, was talking to her gently. She remembered looking at him with vacant eyes, feeling as though she had been violated by him just a moment before. After that incident she was afraid that the same thing might happen if she took the train again. Even thinking about being sick again was enough to bring on nausea.

Reasonably enough, she took a year off high school. Thanks to gradual but serious efforts at rehabilitation, she was somehow able to resume taking the train – but always with the lingering fear that the nausea might break out again.

Finally, six months after going back to school, she decided to switch from her swanky girls school (they had to bow towards the building at the end of the school day!)

to an easier-going co-ed school a bit closer to her house. She cycled to a station about halfway there, then went one station at a time, getting on and off at every stop. About half the week (if her memory of things was correct) she'd be at school from lunchtime, and at least one day a week she would take the day off.

Despite this she still somehow managed to graduate from high school, and by the time she got into college her train-phobia had largely subsided. Thinking back on it now, that was a very happy time for her; she was so busy having fun with her then boyfriend, Yamamoto, a Waseda student, that she didn't have time to get worried about little things. But then again, maybe because she'd been too busy playing around, she'd neglected her studies. So even though it was the tail-end of the eighties economic boom, her attempts to find a job all drew a blank.

"Why in God's name can't you manage to do what everyone else does?"

She put up with the inevitable grumbling of her father, and finally (thanks to a word from a relative) managed to slip into a temporary job at a tabloid paper based in Tsukiji. She ended up getting pregnant by a journalist six years her senior. They got married. The child born was Mika.

But since becoming pregnant with Mika, Natsumi's fear of taking trains had returned.

At first everyone around her said she was just nervous about having her first baby, and Natsumi herself had been prepared to believe it. But even after Mika was safely born there was hardly any change in how she felt. When Mika was still very young, worrying what would happen if she became queasy while carrying a nursing baby made

Natsumi's heart race, so the idea of going somewhere by train never even crossed her mind.

What was bad was that, having been in a situation where she could avoid riding a train if she didn't want to, now Natsumi almost never did, even after Mika had learned to walk. Getting into the habit of never riding a train meant that doing so now seemed even more frightening.

The upshot was that over the last few years she'd gotten worse and worse at taking the train. The last time she'd gotten on a train was at the start of the year, when her father was in hospital in Shibuya. She thought that since it was an emergency it would be okay – but it wasn't. Even though she knew these local Keio Line trains stopped and opened their doors every two minutes, no sooner had it pulled out of the station than the blood drained from her face, the tips of her fingers went cold and numb and she had tumbled out at the next station, unable to bear it.

"I don't know! Which one of you is supposed to be the sick one?" said her flabbergasted mother, drawing close to her husband, seeing how haggard Natsumi looked. In the end Natsumi had taken three taxis one after another (she wasn't too good with taxis either) and somehow made it to the hospital. Of course, it was her hospitalized father who was the really sick one. The proof of this came when he died promptly six weeks later from terminal liver cancer.

3

The minute Natsumi got home Yoshiko rang.

She asked if she could drop by and Natsumi said yes, she

could. Yoshiko lived in the same building two floors above, so was there in less than five minutes.

"Hey," said Natsumi in a deliberately coaxing and sugared voice. "So why is it there aren't women in police boxes?"

It was still only June, but she was pressing a cushion covered in a summery linen to her chest.

"Ha ha, you're such a dummy," replied Yoshiko in the manner of a male ventriloquist, and laughed. "It's obvious. It's because they'd get humped by the male cops in the sleeping quarters upstairs." And she slurped her green tea noisily from a big cup decorated with the name of a sushi shop to commemorate its opening. Of course, Natsumi did have proper teacups for guests, but Yoshiko liked that particular cup.

"Oh, the second floor is for sleeping, is it?"

"That's right – with futons that are never folded away and stink of men. That's the place where the women police officers would be pushed down and poked."

Yoshiko thumped her teacup down on the low *kotatsu* table. Using the fingertips of her right hand she lightly pushed Natsumi's hair back.

"Worse than that, the man would be a fifth *dan* in judo. If you fought back he'd get you in an arm lock and pin you down."

"Eeww! I can't tell Mika that sort of thing," laughed Natsumi as she pushed the cushion against Yoshiko's chest.

"Well, shall I say it for you?"

"Yoshiko, stop it. You're dreadful."

Natsumi frowned winsomely and sipped green tea from her mug. Again it was due to Yoshiko's preference that instead of being in the living room with the sofa, the dining table and the twenty-eight-inch panoramic TV, they were in the little Japanese-style room where a small *kotatsu* served as a low table (of course, since it was not winter right now, the futon had been taken off it). Natsumi and Yoshiko were sitting with their legs stuck out in front of them, which was not the best of manners.

"But is that really the reason?"

"Hmm, who knows..."

Maybe that explanation was just something Yoshiko had come up with to shut her up, because she threw the cushion to one side and drank another sip of tea with a vacant expression on her face. She then bit noisily into a *senbei* rice cracker, the kind baked hard to go well with tea. She didn't say anything else about women police officers to Natsumi.

Not meaning to harp on about it, but Natsumi really knew absolutely nothing about police boxes. She did not know if the policemen in them had dropped into a police station somewhere before coming to work, or if they went to the police box directly from home.

Now that she found herself thinking about what police boxes were like, she did indeed discover that she couldn't imagine one with female police officers in it. If she couldn't picture this scene to herself, she reasoned, it was probably because she had never seen it.

As Natsumi was thinking about this, her daughter Mika – the original cause of her budding obsession with this business – came back from school. Knowing it was nearly time for her return, Natsumi had unlocked the door. She heard the sound of the front door shutting with a bang.

"Hey, Mister-Miss. Have you come to watch the sumo again?"

As she slipped the brand new red satchel off her shoulders, Mika peered into the Japanese room which was right by the entrance.

"Now, now Mika. You know it's naughty to talk like that. And there's no sumo this month anyway."

Mika's cheeks were slightly flushed – perhaps she'd run part of the way home. Natsumi glared at her sternly. She was wearing a short-sleeved red dress and her hair was piled on her head in a little chignon.

"Call Yoshiko by her proper name please."

"Hello, Yoshiko-san." As Mika repeated her greeting, she grinned and tilted her head to one side. It occurred to Natsumi how much like JonBenet Ramsey she looked, but since mentioning that unlucky American's girl's name was likely to put a damper on things she chose to say nothing.

"Hello, Mika," said Yoshiko in a rather more feminine tone than she used when talking to Natsumi. It made Natsumi slightly uneasy to hear Yoshiko with her hair cut short over her ears and in her white polo shirt and silver pants (you had to call them slacks, really) speak that way. "Mika, I hear that recently you've started to get interested in everything to do with police boxes?"

Though the question had been put light-heartedly Mika seemed surprised and went tense for an instant. She then opened her eyes wide and clamped her lips together in a straight line. "Uh-huh," she nodded and went out into the corridor dangling her satchel from one hand.

"Was I wrong to bring it up?"

"No, no. It's no big deal," said Natsumi shaking her head.

Mika came back after a while. She leaned her hand lightly on the pillar in the doorway of the Japanese-style room and smiled an embarrassed smile. She must have gone and dropped off her satchel in her room.

"What's up?"

In response to Natsumi's question, Mika just said all shyly. "Today, you know, I saw a policeman doing his shopping at Seven-Eleven..." Then off she went again, leaving her smile floating in mid-air.

"What's gotten into that kid?" said Natsumi laughing. Yoshiko laughed too.

"Right," Yoshiko said about an hour later. "Me, I'm out of here." She used a masculine pronoun for "I" which went well with her strapping physique.

After Yoshiko had left, Natsumi frantically applied herself to preparing dinner. In fact, the main dishes were all the pre-cooked things she had bought at the market. Just that and nothing else would be a bit sad, so Natsumi decided to make some *tsukune* meat balls which Mika liked. She ground minced chicken in a bowl and rolled it into small balls in the palm of her hand. Mika (who had either an excellent nose or excellent intuition) came into the kitchen and showed how happy she was by yelling "Meat balls! Meat balls!" Mika was so happy and excited that she started making funny noises and pressing herself against Natsumi's check-apron-covered legs like a playful puppy.

"You're getting in my way. That's enough now," laughed Natsumi. But she let Mika gambol around her and even spoke a bit about police boxes. This made Mika even happier.

Once dinner and the bath were done with, Natsumi rang

her husband in Aomori. Together she and Mika sang 'Happy Birthday' in the style of Marilyn Monroe and wished Daddy a happy thirty-fifth birthday.

4

The next day Natsumi went to a police box.

Of course, she hadn't purposely set out to go there; she'd gone to a big stationery shop to buy a new ink ribbon for her word processor as hers had run out (she needed a ribbon because she'd got a job transcribing an interview from a tape for a sumo magazine) and it just happened that there was a police box on the way. This police box was on the Koshukaido road quite near the apartment and it was still in Suginami Ward. It was the kind of building she'd normally not have given a moment's thought to, but when she came to think about it, there really were police boxes all over the place.

The Suginami Ward police box was much older than the Setagaya Ward police box she'd seen yesterday. She didn't know whether it was just chance that this particular police box was like that, or if it was somehow related to the status of the two wards. Both buildings were made of the same raw concrete, but the façade of the windowless second floor of the Setagaya Ward police box was curved, while the left-hand side of the first floor was a plate glass window above a low concrete wall. It occurred to Natsumi now that it did have a certain chic, whereas the Suginami police box was no more than an inelegant and blocky concrete box, with two sliding glass doors side by side serving as the first floor entrance.

She looked up at the smoked-glass windows of the second floor. The place looked like a cheap hotel or flat – definitely not the kind of place you could send women police officers to work in. And sure enough, inside there was a single horribly serious-looking young police*man*.

The horribly serious-looking young police man was sitting at the desk in the middle of the room. He was busy working on what looked like a test book; perhaps he was studying for an exam to get a promotion? This idea suddenly flashed into Natsumi's head although she had not the faintest idea what rank this policeman was or how one went about getting promoted. Standing next to a white bicycle parked by the police box, she nervously peered inside.

The policemen (she really wanted to nickname him "Bookworm") seemed to be grappling with his book of exam questions with intense and unswerving concentration. The inside of the police box was drab; bar the desk there was nothing of any size or substance. There was a little whiteboard up on the wall. From this hung a holder improvised from a wire coathanger, and on it was stuck a roll of low quality, cheap-looking toilet paper. Must be used instead of tissues, thought Natsumi to herself, but to be frank, it looked really tacky. But then – perhaps because they wanted to brighten the mood when you got up close – the cuddly police mascot was displayed in the window, facing outwards and wrapped in a very dusty bit of cellophane.

The mascot was about fifty centimeters tall. Its body was orange and it had on the same black belt bandolier and belt that policemen wear. It held its arms open and was smiling fit to burst. The head made up at least two-fifths of the whole; the shape of the face was similar to ToppoGigio, the Italian mouse, but the ears were slightly longer. The eyes were unnaturally large in the style of Osamu Tezuka characters. Something like an antenna or the lantern part of an anglerfish stuck out from the top of its head, which was the only part that was pale blue.

This was Pin-Pon.

Natsumi recalled having seen this same mascot somewhere else that was definitely not a police box. But at that very moment someone spoke to her from behind so she didn't have the time to dig deeply at all.

"What seems to be the problem?"

Natsumi wheeled around, panicked by the brusque tone of the voice. A policeman stood there, pushing his white bicycle. He must have just come back from a patrol of the neighborhood. Unlike Bookworm inside, he was handsome, even slightly cool-looking. He didn't look like a policeman at all.

"Oh...er. Nothing, nothing at all," replied Natsumi replied in her friendliest manner, and started to walk off hunched forward. From time to time she looked back, laughing unnaturally and bowing her head. The policeman stood rooted to the spot, his cap at a slightly rakish angle on his head, looking after her with a completely mystified air.

"Oh, Mika, Mommy understands now. It's that cuddly toy, Pin-Pon, that you like, isn't it?"

Natsumi was giving Mika dinner in the dining room. She had spoken in a slightly teasing way, but at some point but she had started to enjoy analyzing police boxes.

177

"Mommy, he's called Pi-Po. Not Pin-Pon."

Mika held up her short pink chopsticks in the shape of an X to make it clear that Natsumi was wrong. She was having difficulty picking up the last of the boiled beans that Natsumi had bought at the delicatessen yesterday, chasing them around the plate.

"No, it's not. It's Pin-Pon. Because that's the sound a siren makes"

"No, it's not. It's Pi-Po."

Mika pronounced the name forcefully, pouting as if she were getting a bit angry.

"Yes, yes," said Natsumi. "Of course it's Pi-Po." (Though she didn't believe it and was just humoring her daughter.) She told Mika to use a spoon instead of her chopsticks but Mika refused.

"Mika," Natsumi said coaxingly. "Do you remember when Grandpa died, that mascot was there?"

"Yes, I rememberrrrr."

Perhaps it was because Mika had managed to pick up a bean and was staring at the ends of the chopsticks that she drew out the end of the word. Natsumi giggled.

"At that time you did call him Pin-Pon, you know."

"No, I didn't. His name's Pi-Po."

Mika corrected her mother briskly once more.

After dinner was done, the two of them took a bath together. The tub was small but the water went right up to Mika's chin. She started to count from one to twenty as fast as she could, but seemed to get bored with any number higher than that.

"Mommy," she said, "Tell me about when I was a child." (This although she still was still a child.)

Natsumi was washing herself squatting on the floor of the small bathroom. She couldn't resist teasing her daughter when she was acting all innocent and simple.

"I bought you for a hundred and forty thousand yen at the south annex of Mitsukoshi department store in Shinjuku. It must be about seven-and-a-bit years ago now. You were actually priced at a hundred and seventy thousand, but since it was over three months since you'd been born, they discounted you to a hundred and forty thousand. Yes, Mommy got a great bargain."

"No, I can't believe it," said Mika, sounding as if she was about to burst into tears. Natsumi had expected this kind of reaction. She squeezed Mika's face between her wrists (taking care that her soapy hands didn't touch her), rubbed her nose up against Mika's flat little nose and said, "No, it's not true. It's not true."

5

From the next day on, Natsumi kept up with her observation of police boxes.

At some point she had started to make a circuit of the neighborhood by bicycle. She had gone beyond merely observing – now she was on patrol. Serious. Natsumi wondered what on earth had got into her, but the truth was as she was always doing odd things anyway, she wasn't particularly worried.

On her yellow bicycle with its big shopping basket, Natsumi was about to check out four police boxes in the area she cycled round. Out of these, two were under the control of the police station of Suginami Ward (the ward where Natsumi lived) and the other two were in Setagaya Ward. She did feel that the design of the Setagaya Ward buildings was slightly better, but perhaps there was no great difference after all. If you looked inside, all the police boxes were equally dreary, the police officers were all men, and Pin-Pon (Natsumi now knew that wasn't the right name, but she found it easier to say than Pi-Po) was always smiling at the world outside.

As a result of her daily patrols, Natsumi was gradually getting to know more and more about police boxes. She knew, for example, that on the first floor at the back there was a little room you reached through a small door and that this room contained a sink, a refrigerator and a microwave oven (perhaps the police rested and took their meals in there?).

She had also learned that the consecutive (she thought) numbers and the black characters on the white bicycles parked outside the police box gave the name of the main area police station (this must mean that the officers inside the police box – or rather the police sergeants, this being the rank that got police box jobs as Natsumi had learned at the library – first reported for work at the area police station, and only after that got on their bicycles and came to work. They must have lockers and get changed into their uniforms at the station, and pick up their pistols and truncheons too). She found it easy to remember what the policemen in each police box looked like. If she found anything even faintly distinctive in them, she'd give them a nickname she'd made up (like "Punk," "Mole" and "Smiley"), which seemed to have the amazing effect of making their peculiarities stand out even more.

The thing was that Natsumi could not unveil this knowledge to just anybody. It would be embarrassing. Yoshiko was the exception. Natsumi would report everything to her in great detail. Yoshiko would laugh kindly and say, "What are we going to do with you?" The whole thing was like a game.

It was on the evening of just such a day that Mika declared she wanted to visit the headquarters of the Metropolitan Police Department.

That day when Mika came back from school she didn't go out anywhere to play; nor did she stay in her room laughing aloud as she read her *This is the Police Box in Kameari Park, Katsushika Ward* comic book. She just stayed close to her mother. Perhaps something unpleasant had happened at school, speculated Natsumi. Maybe Mika was having difficulty communicating with her friends. "Would you like to go out for a walk?" proposed Natsumi in her softest, sweetest voice.

"Wouldn't that be nice," said Mika, sounding like a house wife. Then she hesitated a little, declared that she wanted to go the headquarters of the Metropolitan Police Department and burst into tears.

Natsumi was taken aback. She crouched down so that her eyes were level with her daughter's and asked her why she was crying. But Mika's request hadn't surprised her much. You could almost say she'd been expecting it.

"Now, now. There's no need to cry."

Natsumi softly stroked the back of Mika's head. Mika's face went bright red. She whimpered and her nose was running.

"You want to go to the Police HQ?"

"Yes, I do," said Mika in a tearful, pathetic voice. What a pity it would be if Mika's concern for her (knowing she wasn't good at traveling) had prevented her from bringing up the subject. Natsumi felt guilty.

"I bet you saw the poster with Pin-Pon, didn't you?"

Natsumi drew Mika's head towards her, still stroking it gently.

"Mommy, it's Pi-Po. Can't you remember that!" Mika said, still crying. And she jerked her head away from Natsumi quite violently.

"Alright, alright, Pi-Po."

Now Natsumi felt like having a cry herself too. Recently there was a poster on display in police boxes with Pi-Po (she'd decided to call him that from now on) promoting visits to the Police HQ.

Oh no, Natsumi had thought. If Mika saw that, there'd be hell to pay. If they were going to make a poster, why not something a little more dignified, with a photo of a group of police and a slogan like 'Visit us at any time' written in brush-drawn characters. Instead there was Pi-Po inviting people over with his funny face and his arms spread wide. Worse than that, the text was in Q&A format.

'Can I *really* visit the Police HQ?'

'Yes, you can!'

With all that, you didn't need to be Mika to feel tempted to go. (In fact, Natsumi had felt a bit like going herself.). Problem was, Mika seemed to think that if she went to the Police HQ she'd be able to meet the real Pi-Po. Was or wasn't he there? If he wasn't, then that would be a bit of a swindle.

"Okay then, let's go after Daddy's back, okay? We can go by car. Won't that be great?"

Although she'd been feeling guilty about the very same thing just a few seconds ago, without any qualms Natsumi went ahead and used this easy pretext to postpone their visit. It was pathetic but what else could she do? It was a simple fact that it was difficult for Natsumi to take Mika to the Police HQ.

"But Daddy sold our car to Gulliver," said Mika in a slightly peeved tone. (Gulliver was the name of the local second-hand car dealer chain.) Her nostrils flared and she pulled a ghastly face.

"We could rent a car."

"I know Daddy's not coming back."

"Oh yes he is. In August."

"But Mommy, you said that we could go visit Grandpa's grave in August."

"So I did," said Natsumi with an expression that had suddenly turned anxious.

6

From inside the police box the smiling face of Pi-Po was looking at her. Natsumi looked right back at him. She was wearing a bell-shaped beige hat pulled down to her eyes and sticking her lips out in a pout. After holding her stare for several seconds, she burst out laughing.

She pedaled her yellow bicycle off for the next police box. Here you are again, a respectable married woman, out again on your police box patrol. You're getting serious. What's eating you? she asked herself, as she pedaled her bike. She remembered when her father had said to her from his hospital bed, "Come on Natsumi, try and pull yourself together a little." There must definitely be something wrong with a daughter who has such things said to her even after having been married quite a while.

It had been a Saturday in mid-February. She'd picked up Mika from school and taken her to the hospital. Her father was confused. On the previous day he'd just been a little out of sorts, but now all the bed-ridden man could do was open his eyes ever so slightly and babble incoherently.

Natsumi and Mika spent the night in his room. Natsumi's mother stayed over too. Since the heating was turned off at eight o'clock, the room was cold. But they kept warm by using some of the blankets Natsumi's mother had brought in when she'd stayed over before. They took it in turns to rest on the sofa. Only Mika slept on a camp bed a bit like a cheap beach chair.

Her father, who had the needle of his drip stuck into his collarbone, kept up a stream of meaningless muttering. Natsumi strained her ears to listen as she sat on a fold-up metal chair by his bedside and rubbed his swollen legs. Suddenly he lifted up his head and asked dopily if he was dead yet.

"Nope, not dead yet," Natsumi replied laughing softly and in the same light-hearted tone she always used. Her father stared at her with his sunken eyes. Then, in a voice that was horribly clear, he said, "Listen Natsumi, try and pull yourself together a little."

What on earth was the meaning of that comment? Had

he briefly come around, or had his delirium just happened to dovetail with the situation?

Either way, he vomited blood only thirty minutes after that. Natsumi reckoned it was about three o'clock in the morning. There was a little figure hanging from the Y-shaped part of the stethoscope of the young nurse on night-duty – must be the fashionable thing to do. It was orange and it was holdings its hands out, and as the nurse tried to find a heartbeat in her father's chest, it swung and dangled happily in time with her movements.

It was Pi-Po.

A red express train passed through the Keio Line grade crossing.

How strange for all those people who don't even know one another to get into that little box to be carried about. Or maybe there was something strange about her and the way that the more she looked at trains, the less she wanted to take them.

She reached the second police box. A police car was parked in the side street beside it.

That must mean that a detective was paying a visit. Natsumi had made up her mind it must be a detective, but had no real idea who it was really. But, since Natsumi had made up her mind, then a detective it was.

Detectives did sometimes come to visit the police boxes. They wore soft-looking caps with short visors different to the stiff, army-style caps of the policemen on duty at the police box. The cap gave you the impression that their rank was lower than the staff of the police box, but no doubt that was a clever decoy strategy of the kind the police are so good at. The proof was that they always visited the police box in a police car from the main station. That made quite clear the difference in status between them and the officers in the police box, who only rode bicycles.

More than that, the detective would always take the staff of the police box into the back room with him. Yes, that was it. He must be visiting each police box in turn in his patrol car to issue secret orders. The fact was that there was no one in the front of the police box right now. Yes, the detective had come and called the officers into the back room. Within five seconds of having seen the police car parked by the police box, Natsumi had invented her own private and comprehensive explanation of the situation. At this point someone spoke to her.

"Madam?" The voice reminded her of one of those men who come round and try to get you to buy a newspaper subscription. "What are you doing here?"

It's enough to give you a heart attack, to be suddenly spoken to when you're looking at a police box. Why is it then that it's precisely at times like these that people do speak to you? Since the person who'd spoken to her was Yoshiko (who was in the middle of doing her shopping) Natsumi nonchalantly replied "Oh, Yoshiko," and they settled down to continue the observation of the police box together.

She and Yoshiko sat down on the bench of the *taiyaki* bean paste pancake shop diagonally opposite the police box. They crammed the famously fresh-baked and crunchy fish-shaped pancakes into their mouths till their cheeks bulged. Yoshiko not only had a manly physique, but was a hundred and seventy centimeters tall too. Balancing on the backless wooden bench, her mouth stuffed with *taiyaki*, she looked incongruous, deliciously comic. With her eyes fixed on the apparently empty police box, Natsumi imagined what the detective and the officers might be discussing in the room at the back. Since the Aum Supreme Truth cult used to have a training center in this area, the different ranks probably kept in close contact.

"Look, I'm sorry to ask you this right now..." said Yoshiko sounding relaxed beside her. "But why are you inspecting police boxes like this?"

"I don't know," replied Natsumi simply. "I don't know, but it's interesting to look at them."

"Interesting, huh?"

Yoshiko nodded with emphasis and chewed on her *taiyaki* with relish. Natsumi used her fingers to brush away the bean paste which had stuck to the corners of Yoshiko's mouth. There was a primary school boy whistling nearby who stared when he saw this. It must be about time for school to end, thought Natsumi, I should be getting home. When she checked though it wasn't yet time. The schoolboy was plump and dressed in yellow short pants. He kept on staring at Natsumi and Yoshiko as he walked past them, still whistling ineptly. The song was – maybe – *Melody Fair*.

"Tell me," said Natsumi, in a wheedling tone as she bumped her shoulder against Yoshiko's far sturdier shoulder. "Do you think of me as being on the same mental level as Mika?"

Yoshiko tipped her head to one side and still chewing intently said, without a trace of irony, "Oh no. I mean, you're more serious about this than Mika is."

After they'd finished their *taiyaki*, Natsumi left Yoshiko

(as she'd expected, the detective had emerged from the back room) and set off for the next police box.

No matter how hard Natsumi thought about it, she had no idea why she'd started to find police box-watching interesting. But interesting it was – and that was enough.

There were two officers standing in front of the third police box, so Natsumi just pedaled straight past. They were "Eyebrows" and "Touchy-Feely." The eyebrows of "Eyebrows" met in the middle, while "Touchy-Feely" always stood very, very close to the other policemen. It was "Eyebrows" who had the job of standing on guard while "Touchy-Feely" (who didn't want to be apart from him) just kept him company. Thanks to adopting this system of classifying them with nicknames, Natsumi had recently become more and more of an expert in the different officers in each police box. Of course, she also knew plenty about their work. She knew so much it seemed a pity that she didn't have the opportunity to share her knowledge. (She thought that one day she could send in a story to the Asahi newspaper's 'Voices' column.)

Natsumi presently arrived at the fourth police box on her yellow bicycle. No sooner had she thought to herself, "Well, that brings today's patrol to an end," than she noticed a slight difference. What could it be? What had changed? It was like doing a 'Spot the Difference' test. Staring at the inelegant Suginami Ward police box, she quickly figured out the nature of the change. Once you were aware of it, it was actually not a small thing, but quite a big one.

Pi-Po, the mascot who was always there smiling out at the world, was nowhere to be seen.

Wondering if it hadn't just been moved somewhere,

Natsumi looked inside. The officer whom she'd christened "Hairy Boy" was puttering around by himself. There was no sign of Pi-Po. Just then she heard "Hairy Boy" (with his long sideburns and his dark stubble) shout in the direction of the backroom, "Hey, Pi-Po's not here. Where's he gone?" Another officer, "Jowls," emerged lazily from out back and replied "Eh? No idea. Should be there," in a thick accent that Natsumi couldn't place. Natsumi trembled all over when she realized that Pi-Po had been stolen. She had been witness to a rather extraordinary situation: a robbery in a police box. She wanted to stay and watch forever.

If she stayed where she was there was a chance suspicion would fall on her, so she withdrew to a distance of about five meters from the police box. "Hairy Boy" stuck his head out of the police box, and surveyed the area, his eyes darting this way and that. I'm safe, thought Natsumi to herself, surveying the situation from a little way off. She set off home, feeling as if her brain had been secreting some happiness-inducing substance. Given that she'd been making her observations every day, she felt entitled to this sort of dramatic change from time to time. How would things develop? Ooh, it was so exciting! She couldn't wait till the next day. After dinner she'd take a walk with Mika to see what was going on.

Mika as well would probably get excited if she found out that Pi-Po had been stolen. Since Natsumi had ended up being very non-committal in response to Mika's wish to go to the Police HQ, this might buoy her up a bit. When she got back to her apartment block she took her bicycle up to the apartment in the elevator. The door was unlocked; apparently Mika was already back. Her yellow sneakers decorated with moons and stars were in the hall, toe touching toe, where she'd kicked them off.

"Mika, you were early back today, huh?" said Natsumi in the direction of Mika's room as she pushed her bicycle into the hallway. Taking off her low-heeled slip-on shoes, she walked barefoot along the parquet floor of the corridor and knocked on the door of Mika's room. She opened the door just as Mika replied with a drawn-out "Come in."

The western-style room was so small that an American would probably have mistaken it for a closet. Mika was seated on the child-size bed. Natsumi found herself on the verge of crying out like a character from the Peking opera. Perhaps Mika had never intended to hide it; perhaps she'd just decided to bite the bullet because she knew she'd never be able to keep it hidden. Either way, she was clutching a large Pi-Po doll with no attempt at concealment.

"Hairy Boy" turned out to be a nice guy. When Natsumi took Mika to return Pi-Po, he said gently to Mika. "You like Pi-Po, do you? Still that doesn't mean that you can go take him away like that." He spoke like the presenter of the children's aerobics program on TV.

He went so far as to say that if she wanted to see Pi-Po, she could drop in whenever she wanted.

"I hope he's not a pedophile," thought Natsumi suddenly as she watched him. This tasteless notion came partly because she'd relaxed after realizing he wasn't going to make a big issue of the thing.

With his long sideburns and dark stubble, the officer turned to Natsumi. "Madam, this is just a childish prank," he said and let them go without even asking for their names or addresses. Natsumi made Mika say she was sorry again, apologized herself, then left the police box. It may not have blown up into a big issue, but the police now knew her face, meaning that from now on it would be harder for her to get up close to this police box. That was a pity, but there was nothing she could do about it. She'd just have to make do with the other two police boxes.

As they made their way back to their apartment building, Mika seemed to be worrying about how her mother would react. She held onto the hem of Natsumi's linen skirt and dragged her feet a little as she walked.

"What happens when you steal things from other people?" said Natsumi, turning to look at Mika.

Mika looked uneasily back up at her mother and replied faintly, "You get caught by the police."

"And is it alright to steal?"

"No, it's wrong," came Mika's reply.

"I'm glad you understand that," said Natsumi and gave a little laugh. "The police are quite frightening, you know. They can do all sorts of things – like listening in on you."

And off she went, saying various things which there was very little point saying to a child. Then she put her hand on Mika's as it gripped her skirt and pulled it towards her. Her skirt quickly resumed its shape where Mika had been holding it. Their hands were loosely interlinked.

"So Mika," asked Natsumi, glancing at the road beside her, "do you want to go the Police HQ?" The Koshukaido was a major road with four lanes in each direction. It was two-thirds covered by the umbrella-like elevated expressway running above it. Mika did not reply. Perhaps she hadn't heard. Looking at Mika, Natsumi asked the same question again.

"I do want to go," she replied feebly.

"Oh well, that's settled then." Natsumi made up her mind to talk to Yoshiko the next day. Though she only used it to go shopping at the local Inageya supermarket, Yoshiko did in fact own a red SUV with a big bumper up front.

"Why me for Chrissake?" protested Yoshiko, sounding very masculine indeed, but finally agreed to take them. Natsuki said how grateful she was and promised she wouldn't make any trouble. Since she'd stopped taking trains it had become hard for her to believe that central Tokyo was actually there on the other side of Shinjuku. For her, Tokyo terminated abruptly at that point. For all she knew Tokyo stopped there and became a waterfall (and for all she knew Tokyo was supported on the back of an elephant).

"You're crazy," said Yoshiko, sporting a pair of prescription-lens Rayban sunglasses. "If the roads are empty we'll be in Sakuradamon in forty or fifty minutes." It was a weekday in early July. Yoshiko was driving her car (which she adored) and Natsumi and Mika were in the back seat.

Through her dark red polo shirt, Yoshiko's broad shoulders exuded reliability. No way could anyone think of her as the average housewife. But even so, Natsumi (who was no good at traveling in vehicles of any kind) kept pestering her for breaks until she stopped the car. Every time the car stopped, Mika, who was wearing her favorite blue dress (she'd worn it the day before yesterday too) would open up her *This is the Police Box in Kameari Park, Katsushika Ward* comic book and, though she wasn't actually able to read all the kanji characters properly, would snigger a little strangely to herself. Natsumi was irritated by her daughter being so well-prepared and she prodded the end of her nose and teasingly said "Hey there, Pi-Po thief." Mika stopped laughing immediately and burst into tears. Natsumi then made desperate efforts to soothe her, apologizing repeatedly, while Yoshiko laughed and called her "a hopeless mother."

In Shinjuku they parked the car in a metered lot and the three of them went for a wander near the Tokyo Metropolitan Government Building. Whichever way they went, they were still close to the Tokyo Metropolitan Building. This made them feel a bit like the proverbial monkey Songoku riding on the palm of Buddha, but for the three of them it was a bit of fun.

In the end it took them two-and-a-half hours to get to the Sakuradamon Police HQ in Yoshiko's car. At the end they were cutting things rather fine. When they set out, they'd reckoned it would take just under three hours, so they were just in time to catch the start of the tour. Meanwhile Natsumi was approaching her limit for being stuck in a car. Yoshiko declared that she was going to turn off the willow-lined road by the Imperial Palace moat and look for a parking place. She dropped them off at Iwaita-bashi bridge, two traffic lights before Sakuradamon. Holding Mika by the hand, Natsumi walked along, looking to the right where the Imperial Palace was surrounded by gardens and water.

"Mika, what day is it today?" asked Natsumi, noticing that her daughter was anxiously looking up at her.

"It's Foundation Day," replied Mika, looking a little embarrassed. But really it was just any old Tuesday.

7

The Police HQ was in a building about fifteen floors tall. It had towers on the roof that looked like the candles (rather on the thick side, it must be said) on a birthday cake.

Ms. Kuramochi was already waiting outside the front entrance. A schoolmate of Natsumi's from junior high school, Ms. Kuramochi was now the editor of a mail order magazine. Why was she there? Because they'd sort of vaguely decided on it while chatting on the phone. It was this vague affinity between them that explained how they'd been friends such a long time. In fact, the tour reservation had been made by Ms. Kuramochi, who was used to making all kinds of appointments for work.

"It's been ages. Mika, how you've grown!" she said.

Though she dressed conservatively, Ms. Kuramochi was an enthusiastic collector of character goods. She had actually come to Police HQ in order to buy Pi-Po merchandise. Ms. Kuramochi's apartment, in which she lived alone, was overflowing with Kero the frog, Koro the dog and Sato the elephant. She'd apparently been told it wasn't too healthy when she went to the class reunion for the first time in ten years last year. Since Natsumi hadn't gone herself, she didn't know exactly what had happened there (or, for that matter, what had been said about her on that occasion).

The meeting time was two-thirty.

The uniformed policeman standing in front of the glass-fronted entrance hall kept looking their way. He wore a blue shirt, navy pants and a stiff cap just like the officers in the police boxes. Two or three people, probably more visitors for the tour, exchanged some words with him, then drifted inside. Yoshiko, who'd managed to park the car, arrived at two-thirty on the dot. She was hurriedly introduced to Ms. Kuramochi, then they headed for the entrance.

"You must be the Kuramochi group," said the uniformed policeman even before they had given him their name. He looked at Yoshiko a little longer than any of the others and muttered as if assuring himself, "That is a woman, right." They did as he said and went into the lobby where the other visitors had assembled. Another policeman came over.

"Ms. Kuramochi of Shibuya ward? Four people, isn't it?" Ms. Kuramochi looked a little spooked.

"What's wrong?" inquired Natsumi.

"I told them the name of my company, but I never told them my address," Ms. Kuramochi whispered back.

It wasn't clear whether he'd overheard or not, but a slightly cocky smile hovered around the policeman's mouth before he went off.

We've come to a rather scary place, though Natsumi. Or maybe it wasn't.

Just then a young woman with pink lip gloss appeared.

"Okay, I'll be your guide today," she declared in a bright voice, like the presenter of a TV sing-along for kids (whichever way you looked at it though, Mika was the only elementary school child there).

The woman was wearing a short-sleeved blue shirt and a tight navy blue skirt. Referring to the list she was holding, she began a roll call of the visitors. She confirmed the names and the number of people then handed out pins from an old Yoku Moku cookie tin.

"Anyone under junior high school age doesn't need to

wear a pin," she said.

This meant that Mika couldn't get one. The blue rectangular pin showed Pi-Po flying through the sky. Mika started tugging insistently on Natsumi's one-piece dress saying "Mommy, I want one!"

"Okay," said Natsumi. "You put on mine." She was about to hand hers over when she was told off. "Madam, you must wear it," said the woman (whose hair was very short, in an old-fashioned 'Cecile' cut). Her voice was gentle, but had the hint of an authority that you could not fight against.

"Mika, we can go to the souvenir shop later," said Ms. Kuramochi in an effort to comfort her.

8

A group of three girls all with the same dyed brown hair; five junior high school boys with white open-neck shirts, black trousers and shaven heads; a sixty-year old man with his daughter in her thirties; a woman in her twenties with pageboy hair and thick glasses. God knows why they were there, but there were about a dozen visitors in addition to Natsumi's group.

"Right. Follow me, please."

When the policewoman with the very short hair gave the word, they all started to troop off.

"The interior of this building is like a maze, so please do not wander off," said the policewoman by way of explanation. No sooner did she say this than everyone felt they were in the depths of a labyrinth. They went past the reception desk deeper inside the building. Their guide led them up some stairs (they were a weird triangular shape) and into a room on the second floor. It was just like a preparatory school classroom, with desks and benches lined up and a big video projector up towards the front.

The policewoman distributed some flimsy brochures with the words "Welcome to the Headquarters of the Metropolitan Police" in a mixture of Japanese and English on the cover. She told them the rules; and she also told them the building was not just a tourist facility but included working interrogation rooms and holding cells. This meant it was a bit of a maze, so visitors were not permitted to go wherever they pleased. There was only one restroom in a specified place that they could use. She would show them where it was, otherwise they couldn't go and so on and so forth. Then she left the room.

"Heavy stuff! Can't even take a pee when I want to," said Yoshiko after the woman had left.

"Probably even locked the door of the room, bitch" chimed in Ms. Kuramochi, tailoring her register to match Yoshiko's vulgarity. Mika begged Natsumi to show her the visitor's pin she'd clipped to the shoulder strap of her dress and tried to pull it off.

"Mika," repeated Ms. Kuramochi, "we'll go to the souvenir shop later."

The woman officer returned, timing her arrival to coincide with the end of the video about the structure of the police force. Then off they went to have a look at the archive room on the same floor. There were glass cases like the ones used to display jewels in jewelers. Inside they saw the gun permit of a serial killer who had used a rifle for his crimes; the confession of a man who'd murdered five housewives; and a knife that had been used for a crime.

They took a souvenir photo with them clutching a Pi-Po doll the same size as the one in the police boxes, and then their time was up for that part of the tour. The restrooms that visitors could use were near the archive room, but none of them needed to go. Since the short-haired woman had spoken to her in a friendly way, Natsumi ventured to ask her a question.

"Come to think of it, do *you* know if there are any women police officers in police boxes?"

At exactly the same time, the woman officer gave a little nod and started moving off. Natsumi did not feel it was worth calling her back, so the question was left up in the air.

"I think there are some police boxes with women officers who know sign-language," Ms. Kuramochi said. But they all agreed that basically it was the domain of men. Since you often see women police officers in mini police cars, that must means they do more traffic-related work.

"That's discrimination, that is," said Yoshiko, though it wasn't clear if she meant it or not. "In soaps on TV there are always plenty of women detectives."

"What's discrimination?" asked Mika.

"Something that's bad," Natsumi replied in typical motherly autopilot mode.

Another roll call was taken after they left the archive room. "And now, ladies and gentlemen," Miss Officer Shortilocks said. "What you've all been waiting for. We shall now visit the communications and control center."

Natsumi was a little startled. She'd not been looking

forward to this especially (in fact she didn't know what they were going to see in the tour). She was even more surprised when Ms. Kuramochi pointed to a policeman and said "That one there. He's a sergeant."

"How do you know that?"

"See, he has medals on his chest to indicate his rank. Two vertical stripes means a sergeant. It was one of the displays in the archive room just now," she said rather conceitedly, pointing with her chin to the inside of the room. When could she have seen that? Natsumi realized that her specialty was secretly peeping into the police boxes in her neighborhood. But she became timid when she was dealing with a building on a really big scale.

They were going to use the elevator to get up to the communications and control center on the fifth floor.

"Even if the buzzer goes off," said the officer somewhat unreasonably, "I still want you all to squeeze in." The door of one of the three elevators finally opened. It was already full of people. Natsumi assumed that it wouldn't be possible for them all to get in, so they'd just let it go.

"Alright, everyone in, please. Even if the buzzer goes off, get in," instructed the woman officer, driving them in. The buzzer had already gone off by the time the father and daughter and three girls with dyed brown hair had got in.

"Come along. Quickly now."

The woman managed to get the group of schoolboys, the woman with glasses, Ms. Kuramochi and Yoshiko into the elevator. The buzzer was still going off (she said it didn't mean there were too many people, just that the doors were about to close, though that was probably a fib). In the elevator people were jam-packed together. There was no way that any more people could get in, but the woman officer, her pink-painted lips in a pout, said "Come along. Inside please."

It was like a rush-hour train, thought Natsumi. Suddenly she couldn't do it. Suddenly her heart started racing.

"In you go now."

Pressed like this, Natsumi held Mika's hand and got in full of dread. Inside the elevator she'd been pushed into was the tour group plus some middle-aged men wearing suits that reeked of mothballs. The woman officer joined them and the doors slowly shut.

"IwanttogetoutIwanttogetout." Natsumi's hands clenched.

"That hurts," said Mika uneasily.

They had only gotten to the third floor, but the doors of the elevator opened.

"I'm getting out here," said a relaxed male voice from the corner.

Before the man who'd spoken could get out, Natsumi tumbled out. "I'm sorry, I just can't take the elevator anymore," she said to the officer who was still inside. She realized that Mika, whose hand she was holding and who had gotten off with her, was staring up at her.

"What is the matter with you?" asked the woman officer looking surprised. Several people stepped out to let out the man who had spoken a moment before.

"I just can't take the elevator. Let me use the stairs," said Natsumi.

"That's out of the question," said the woman officer curtly. The man in the suit slipped past her and out of the elevator.

In the end everyone in the tour group was made to get out on that floor. The woman ran her eye over them rapidly to confirm they were all there before taking away her hand, which was holding open the elevator doors.

"What's wrong? Are you all right?" inquired Miss Officer Shortilocks with a degree of sympathy as she came up close to Natsumi. But the eyes that sized her up were cold (weren't they?). Natsumi said again that she was feeling sick and wanted to use the stairs. If that was impossible, then she'd drop out of the tour at this point.

"I am not able to permit that," said the officer sternly, her attitude changing abruptly. "Everyone must travel together. That's the rule. So if you drop out of the tour here then it's over for everyone."

"No way!" said one of the junior high school boys, sounding very pissed. His friends nudged him and a laugh ran round the group. The other visitors were all staring at Natsumi now.

"Can't you even take the elevator to the fifth floor?"

"No, I can't."

"Back to the first?"

"No."

"Not at all?"

"No." Natsumi shook her head feebly. She wanted to go home right now. "I think I'm going to throw up..."

"Well this is hopeless." The policewoman frowned. She thought for a while then tilted her head to one side. "Alright then, you wait here for a moment. I'll take everyone else upstairs and then come back for you."

She pressed the button to call the up elevator then turned back to Natsumi and, sounding like a school teacher or someone like that said, "You're as white as a sheet, so just sit down there."

Natsumi and Yoshiko were squatting against the wall in the corner of the narrow elevator lobby like schoolgirls watching a gym class. After all, they'd gotten permission to sit from Miss Officer Shortilocks, hadn't they? They asked Ms. Kuramochi to take Mika with her. People who came to take the elevator looked at them as if to say *what's going on here?* Yoshiko, who was squatting with her knees apart like a suburban punk (or a suburban punk's girlfriend), mouthed the words 'What you looking at?' then whispered in Natsumi's ear that if they ran off right now, a written apology wouldn't be enough to get the policewoman off the hook.

Natsumi laughed softly. "My interest in police boxes got out of control. And look at the mess I'm in now."

The officer came back down in the elevator.

"Do you feel up to using the elevator now?" she asked Natsumi.

"No way," she replied.

That seemed to be the reply she'd been expecting. "Well, let's take the stairs then," she said curtly.

Why didn't you just say that at the beginning then? thought Natsumi, but couldn't bring herself to say it. Walking along a meandering white corridor they were led to a simple staircase, but not the one they'd taken up to the second floor. Simple means it had one set of stairs, a landing, then another set of stairs. The normal zigzag shape, in other words.

The officer was climbing the stairs ahead of Natsumi and

Yoshiko. She turned round briefly and asked, "So you're not good with elevators huh?"

"No kind of transport at all actually," replied Natsumi. Behind her Yoshiko laughed loudly.

When they reached the fifth floor they walked along another meandering white corridor. Halfway along it was a room where the staff were getting physical check-ups. A man and a woman in white coats sat at a reception desk and looked at Natsumi and her entourage with astonishment. They got to the communications and control center (the place that everyone had been dying to see) and the officer unlocked the door (which meant of course that the people inside had been locked in). The policewoman noticed that one of the group – the woman with the pageboy cut – was taking notes. She strode over to examine them with a stern "Any problem over here?" Mika and Ms. Kuramochi walked slowly over to join them.

They were not so much in the communication and control center as a place from which you could observe the communication and control center. It was a long narrow room with a glass wall overlooking the communication and control center below. In the center itself, there were ranks of desks groaning with high-tech equipment and, they were told, the teams of uniform-wearing bods at each desk were busy taking emergency calls. The walls were as high as two or three regular rooms, and on the right was a giant monitor projecting the image of Pi-Po. (The picture must have been chosen for the benefit of the tour group.) On the left there was a map (it was even bigger than the screen) of the whole of Tokyo. On this map were hundreds of shining red lights. If you looked carefully, you could see that from time to time they moved. Apparently this told you the location and direction of travel of all the police cars in Tokyo. That was truly amazing. Could they really keep track of them all? As for Mika, she was smiling as she gazed down at Pi-Po on the monitor.

Natsumi used the stairs to get down to the first floor. They went down the same zigzag-shaped stairs they'd come up. Miss Officer Shortilocks who was walking down in front of her, gave a tight-lipped smile and said, "This is the first time I've ever done this."

Her tone seemed to suggest that she could not believe that people like Natsumi actually existed. No, it was wrong for Natsumi to imagine she felt like that: Shortilocks after all was being a good-natured guide.

"I'm so sorry," was Natsumi's weak reply.

On the first floor they hooked up with the rest of the group. That was the end of the tour. They didn't go to the souvenir shop. They did not know if that was because Natsumi's little crisis had eaten into the time and the shopping had been cut out of the tour, or because it was not part of the original plan. Either way, it was three-thirty on the nose when they emerged outside. Mika was disappointed and grumbled, "Is that all I get to see of Pi-Po?"

In her annoyance that she hadn't made it to the souvenir shop, Ms. Kuramochi was muttering about what an unpleasant atmosphere the Police HQ had. They were all feeling pissed off one way or another.

The four of them strolled over to Hibiya Park where Yoshiko had left the car.

"Did Mommy make a fool of herself?" Natsumi asked Mika.

"Uh-uh, not really," she replied.

A young man dressed in a suit was running along the road next to the moat. There was so much greenery you couldn't see inside the Imperial Palace at all. They went into Hibiya Park and bought some lukewarm lemonade at a booth and drank it sitting in a row on a big white bench. Natsumi daydreamed about one scenario: what would have happened if she and Yoshiko had knocked down Miss Officer Shortilocks on the narrow staircase coming down from the third floor and Ms. Kuramochi and Mika had taken over the communications center and kept the other visitors hostage there. If they'd succeeded, it would have definitely caused quite a rumpus.

But no, thought Natsumi, that's not really me, is it? That's more of a Yoshiko-like scheme. And anyway, whatever happens I'll never get the chance to do it. They're probably already working on new guidelines for what to do when a visitor like me turns up on the tour.

"'My name is Pi-Po.'" To Natsumi's right, Ms. Kuramochi had succumbed to Mika's begging and was reading aloud from the brochure they'd been given at the Police HQ. "'I was named from the 'Pi' sound of People and the 'Po' sound of police.' It's English. Do you understand?"

"No, I don't," answered Mika, as she crossed and uncrossed her legs. On Natsumi's left, Yoshiko was peering at her through the green lemonade bottle.

Ms. Kuramochi declared that she had to get back to her office and left. After she'd gone, it suddenly occurred to Natsumi what a nice flower-pattern skirt she'd been wearing. She looked up at the clear sky in which a single cloud shaped like an air ship was floating slowly by. When she thought about the earth turning she felt afraid. It would be really pathetic for a twenty-nine-year-old like her never to be able to take an elevator. From her Miffy handbag Mika extracted the newest volume of *This is the Police Box in Kameari Park, Katsushika Ward* and opened it on her lap.

"There's no need to be afraid of anything," said Yoshiko beside her in a hypnotic voice.